Kelvedon Hatch, 1840 – 1920:

A Guided Tour

Kelvedon Hatch, 1840 – 1920:

A Guided Tour

By Phil George

History House

Kelvedon Hatch, 1840-1902: A Guided Tour
copyright © 2014 Philip George

The moral rights of the author have been asserted.

All rights reserved. No part of this publication may be reproduced, distributed, or transmitted in any form or by any means, including photocopying, recording, or other electronic or mechanical methods, without the prior written permission of the publisher, except in the case of brief quotations embodied in critical reviews and certain other non-commercial uses permitted by copyright law.

Published by
History House
15 Kelvedon Green
Kelvedon Hatch
Brentwood
Essex
CM15 0XG

historyhouse.co.uk

First published 2014

ISBN: 978-1-291-81768-3

Contents

Author's Note and Acknowledgements	7
Map of parish boundaries in 1840 and 2014	8
Introduction	9
The Enclosure of the Common	11
Population and Employment	12
Introduction to the Tour	13
Part 1 - The Windmill to Hatch Farm via Eagle Lane, Mill Lane, and School Road	14
Part 2 - St Nicholas' Church and then south along the Ongar Road to Well Cottage	38
Part 3 - From the White House, south along the Ongar Road to Brizes	52
Part 4 - From Pheasant Lodge to Rose Cottage on the Ongar Road, via Frog Street	60
Part 5 - Old Crown Lane to Green Lane and Crown Road	71
Part 6 - Dodds Farm to Kelvedon Hall Cottages via Church Road and Beacon Hill	77
Part 7 - Kelvedon Hall, St Nicholas' Church (old and new) Langford Bridge Farm, Great Myles, Pump House Farm, the Rectory and Priors	84
Part 8 - Swan Lane to Blackmore Road and Stocks Lane	106
Selected Bibliography	120
Notes	121

Author's Note and Acknowledgments

Since moving to Kelvedon Hatch in 1987, I have been interested in its history. I was particularly inspired by the collection of photographs assembled by Harold Watts (1922 - 2004). Living in the parish since 1923, he had the foresight to collect photographs of the parish and its inhabitants which probably would have been thrown away in the due course of time. I am fortunate to now have custody of that collection and I would like to thank the people of Kelvedon Hatch, past and present, for their contributions to this collection. I have also received contributions from across the UK, Australia and Canada. Particular thanks go to Julian Gooding, Russ Palmer, Linda Stouffer Hashimoto, John Norris, and the Porter and Curtis families. I would also like to thank Judy Cowan for allowing me to republish some of the photographs from her two interesting books on the history of the village. Since Judy's books were published in 1984 and 1986, many more digital archives have become available, so now is a perfect time to revisit the history of Kelvedon Hatch. I would also like to thank the staff of the Essex Record Office for all their assistance and advice.

Researching local history is like completing a jig-saw puzzle. Most of the edge pieces are still in the box, but many more pieces are missing, especially those relating to women and the working class. Unknowingly, sometimes pieces from another puzzle have been added to the box, and yet they still seem to fit and are not always recognised as being from another jig-saw and rejected. The end result is a picture with a few confusing details and many blank spaces. Despite all these difficulties, it is hoped that this particular puzzle will give a clear picture of the parish over 100 years ago.

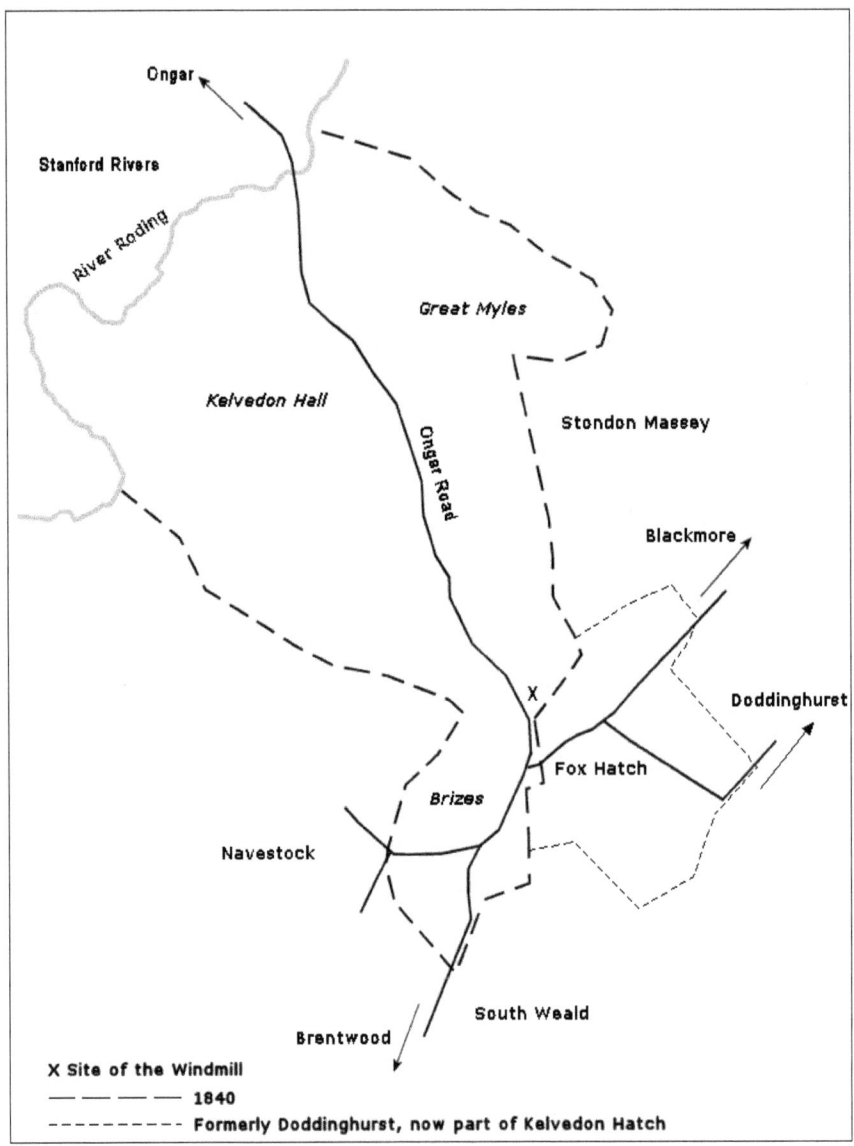

Fig. 1. Map showing the parish boundaries in 1840 and 2014; adjacent parishes; main roads; principal estates in 1840; and the site of the windmill, the starting point of the tour.

Introduction

On a dark November night in 1841, a farm labourer was making his way home across Kelvedon Common with his wages of eleven shillings in his pocket. The common was a dark and lonely place to walk at night. A light in a window of one of the cottages surrounding the common could barely be seen and would certainly not help light his way. Suddenly he was accosted by four robbers who demanded his money. He handed it over but at the same time pleaded with them that he had no food at home for his wife and family. He must have been successful as the leader of the gang begrudgingly directed one of his companions to hand back a shilling. This was done and the labourer made his way home, at least fortunate not to have suffered any injury.

Upon reaching home, he found his wife and in front of her flung down the coin on the table exclaiming that was all he had for his week's earnings as he had been robbed. Both must have been equally surprised for there on the table lay a gold sovereign. Perhaps the proceeds of an earlier robbery, in the darkness the robber had picked the wrong coin from his pocket and presented the happy labourer with nine shillings profit.[1]

This unknown labourer would soon witness a change in the landscape of the common. The common land with its gorse and bracken would disappear following enclosure, and during the next 130 years part of the former common would become the site of the present day village of Kelvedon Hatch. This book explores the early development of the village and goes on a tour of the parish as it was during the nineteenth and early-twentieth centuries. With the help of photographs, newspapers and documents from the archives, the story of some of its inhabitants and the houses in which they lived will be revealed.

Complicating the guide is the fact that the parish boundary was changed in the late-twentieth century when Kelvedon Hatch parish took over part of the parish of Doddinghurst. Therefore, this book will also include information about part of the former Doddinghurst parish known as Fox Hatch and which bordered on the common.

The name Kelvedon Hatch appears in early documents with many different spellings including Kelweduna, Kylewendune, Kilewendune, and Killeuenduna, to name a few. Duna is Saxon for a hill. Kelwe (and its variations) is more problematical. It is thought to mean spotted or speckled. In the case of Kelvedon Hatch this may refer to the colour of the trees in autumn, but most likely, it refers to the soil which in places has large deposits of pebbles mixed in with it, dumped here by the glaciers during the last ice age.

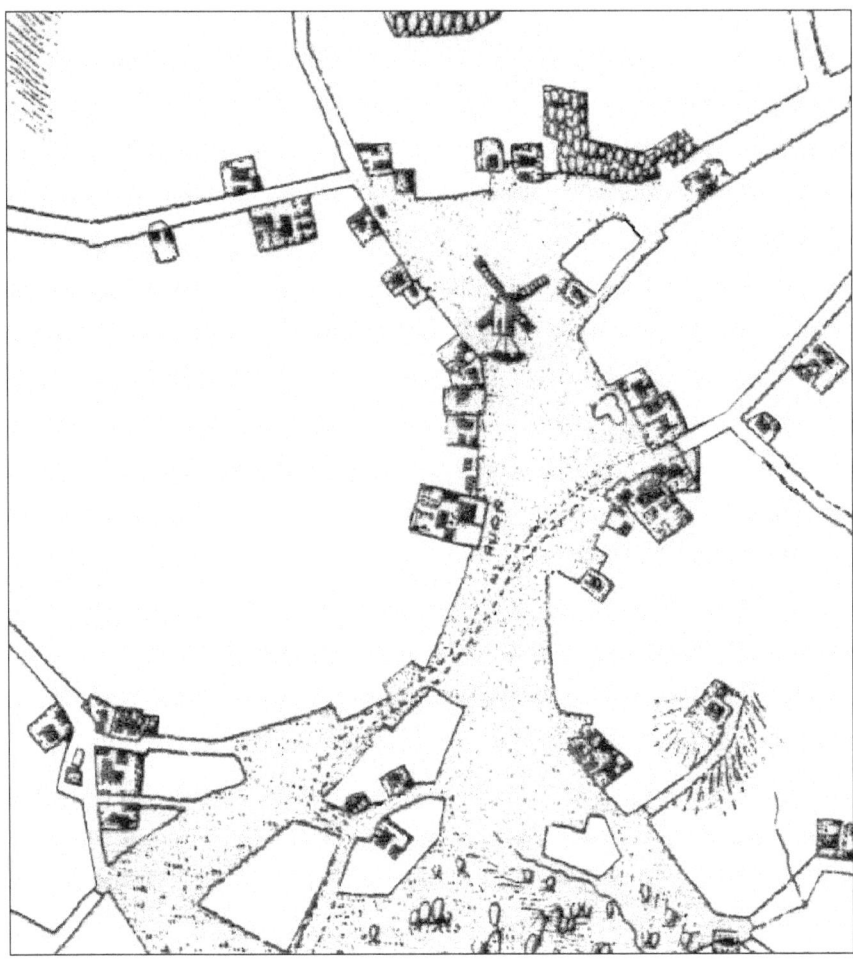

Fig. 2. Map of the common adapted from Chapman and Andre's map, 1777.

Hatch is derived from the Old English word 'haecc', meaning gate.[2] Therefore, the Hatch part of the name refers to gates which were erected on the roads to stop animals straying off the common. It had been added to the name by the thirteenth century. Medieval land ownership records reveal that living near these gates were Hugo de Hec (1248)[3] and Radulpho atte Hacche (1327).[4]

Kelvedon Hatch was also known to the inhabitants as Keldon. The manor of Kelvedon Hall was called Keldon Hall and there are references to Keldon in the parish magazine. Similarly, the name of Kelvedon Common was shortened to Keldon Common. References to the name Keldon are far fewer in the early-twentieth century, probably because of increased population movement. It is now no longer used.

The Enclosure of the Common

Prior to the end of the nineteenth century, the population of the parish was scattered. In the north of the parish were the eighteenth-century mansions of Great Myles and Kelvedon Hall (with the parish church next to it) and a few scattered houses and farms. In the south was the common land dominated by a windmill. On the west side of the common, the Kelvedon Hatch side, were a number of cottages and houses, including Brizes, another eighteenth-century mansion. On the east side in Doddinghurst parish were more cottages and houses. Running through the parish from north to south was the main Ongar to Brentwood road, and branching off on the common were roads to Blackmore, Stondon Massey, and Navestock.

Chapman and Andre's map of 1777 (Fig. 2) is the first detailed map of the area prior to the enclosures. The common land and the windmill are clearly shown. The windmill was sited a short distance from the present-day water tower in Mill Lane. Most of those who lived in the cottages and houses surrounding the common worked on the estates of the great mansions or on nearby farms, or were engaged in providing goods and services such as blacksmiths, wheelwrights, grocers and publicans. Those living around the common were sometimes disparagingly referred to as 'the commoners'.

The principal landowners at this time were the Wrights of Kelvedon Hall; the Dolbys and later the Roydses of Brizes; the Fanes of Great Myles; and the Waldegraves of Navestock. Other individuals owned smaller properties, held either as freehold or copyhold of the manor.

From 1777 onwards, small enclosures were made on the common for new houses and cottages; and in 1831, part of the common consisting of 3 acres was enclosed by the trustees of the lord of the manor of Kelvedon Hall. For a small annual payment, parishioners could use the land as allotments to grow potatoes, cabbage and other vegetables.[5] These allotments came to be called the 'Common Gardens'.[6] Another enclosure took place when an anonymous donor paid for a piece of the common adjoining the existing Poor's Field to be added to the 'Poor's Charity'.

In 1836 it was decided that the remainder of the Kelvedon Hatch side of the common would be enclosed. With the agreement of all the copyholders, the last 54 acres were surveyed and mapped on behalf of the lord of manor. Copyholders were each granted a piece of the common. Some had the land surrounding their property enlarged to include parts of the former common; while others gained possession of plots on the common which could then be hedged and turned to agriculture, or, as happened later, house building. In exchange, the copyholders lost their right to commonage. Commonage included the right to graze their animals on the common. The loss of this did not affect in any great way the owners of the properties, but it did affect their working-class tenants who enjoyed the same right. Over 100 years later, the anger of the commoners over the enclosure and loss of their rights was still being passed down the generations.[7]

During the next few years, the common was marked out and planted with quickset hedges.[8] A few remaining sections of the hedging can still be seen as you walk through the village today. It was not, however, a swift process of enclosure for all the common. It was not until 1858 that the lord of the manor of Doddinghurst made an agreement with the Doddinghurst copyholders that the 34 acres on their side of the common would be enclosed.[9]

Population and Employment

A brief look at the population of Kelvedon Hatch will be useful as additional background. The growth and decline of the population of Kelvedon Hatch from 1801 until 1921 followed the trend of other villages in England. Reaching its zenith in 1851, the population then began to decline until 1911. A number of factors caused this decline across rural England: industrialisation; a decline in agriculture; poor wages and conditions in the countryside; and improved communications and transport. For the parish of Kelvedon Hatch, the decline in population may have been greater had it not been for the enclosure of the common land which encouraged the building of new houses.

Detailed analysis of the census returns reveals that between 1841 and 1891 agricultural workers formed a fairly constant presence in the parish of between 49% and 59% of the population. There are similar numbers for their households: between 49% and 60%. It was also a male dominated parish, with many single, young men employed as agriculture workers living among the community as lodgers or boarders. Analysis of the structure of the households of agricultural workers has found that between 1841 and 1891 there was an increasingly aging population, with a decline in the size of households and of the numbers in each family. There was also a reduction in the number of simple family households and the emergence of increasingly extended and multiple family households. In other words, more grandparents were living with their children and helping out in the family home while the parents worked. It is thought that this was for economic reasons and was one effect of the late-Victorian agricultural depression.

The most interesting fact revealed is that while many families left the parish seeking a better life, others remained, and so did their children when they became adults and had their own families. This is clearly displayed by looking at four family names found in the parish and how they make up a large percentage of all the agricultural workers' households.

Family name of head of household	1851	1861	1871	1881	1891
Jarvis	1	2	3	4	3
Enever	3	2	2	5	4
Quilter	1	2	2	2	3
Porter	-	2	3	3	5
Total and as a percentage of all ag. Workers households	5 (9%)	8 (15%)	10 (20%)	14 (29%)	15 (33%)

Kinship must have been an important factor for these families, but it is hard to know the full social or economic factors at work in their decision to stay in the parish.[10] There will be more information about some of these families during the tour.

Introduction to the Tour

During the tour, a property or an individual may be mentioned several times. To assist the reader, each property has been given a unique number and any reference to that property or a person connected with it will be followed by the number in brackets: [ ]. The letter *d.* after the number indicates the property has since been demolished.

Each part of the tour has a map (not to scale) which shows the properties that existed between 1840 and 1920, and the main roads and lanes.

The primary sources for the tour are the ten-yearly census returns, newspaper archives, maps, parish magazines and manorial records. A detailed list of the sources can be found in the bibliography and notes. The census does have its limitations. It is a snap-shot in time - just one night every ten years. A person might be away on the night of the census, or was only staying in the household for a short time. They can also contain errors: deliberate or unintentional. In an attempt overcome these errors, every effort has been made to cross-check the information with other sources. In the census returns the descriptions of occupations were prescribed and limited, and in the case of agriculture, the most common category was 'agricultural labourer'. This all-encompassing term could also include thatchers, hedgers and ditchers, hay-binders, woodmen, cowmen and horsemen. Also, the labourer would be subject to seasonal employment or day labour and would supplement his wages by other work such as road mending or gardening, perhaps in one of the great mansions. Women also worked in agriculture: planting, harvesting and weeding; as did their children. So in this book the more general term of agricultural workers will be used.

Part 1

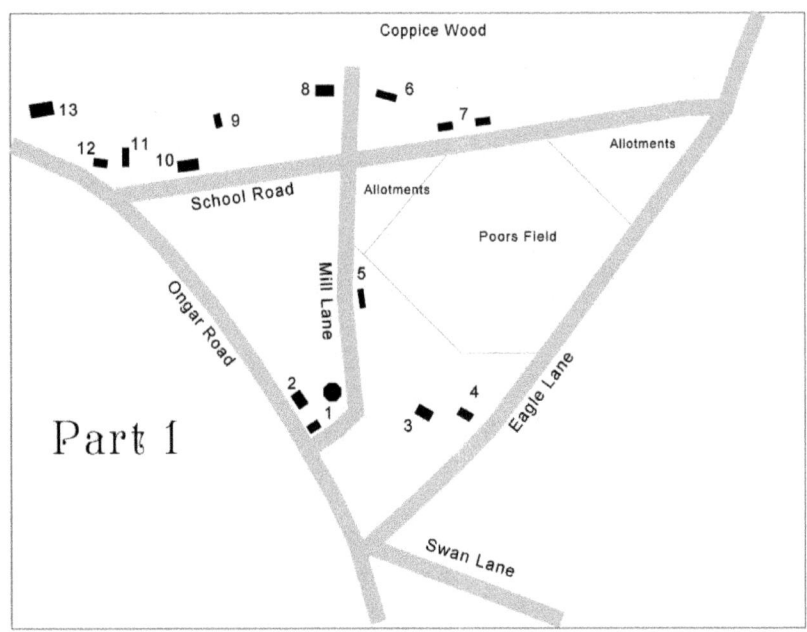

Fig. 3.

Fig. 4. Windmill and Mill Cottage c.1905.

The Windmill and Mill Cottage [1] *d.*

The tour starts at the windmill in what is now Mill Lane. The windmill would have dominated the common as there were few tall trees on the common. The first record of the windmill is from 1644 in the parish registers.[11] Originally a post mill, in the early-nineteenth century it was replaced with a new smock mill: a sloping, horizontally weather-boarded tower with eight sides on a brick ground floor. It was topped with a roof or cap that was rotated by a fan-tail to bring the sails into the wind. The last fan-tail on the windmill came from another windmill at nearby Bentley when it was demolished.[12] The mill could carry 11 yards of cloth, and was capable of grinding ten loads a week and storing 60 quarters of grain.[13][14]

The windmill was owned by the Kelvedon Hall estate and leased to different people during the nineteenth century. Some were themselves millers, while others were local farmers who then sub-let it to millers. In 1830 it was occupied by Richard Woodfine, a miller. During or soon after his tenancy, a cottage was built near the mill. This became known as Mill Cottage and only contained four rooms. Outside there was a wash-house, workshop, and an earth closet.[15]

For some of the tenants, operating the mill was part-time employment. The tenants in the 1840s were Charles Gandy, and then his son, William; both were licensees of the Eagle Inn [24] opposite. In the 1860s, it was Thomas Brown, a blacksmith, who lived in the Red House [17]. The next occupant, however, was a full-time miller. David Rainbird and his family lived in Mill Cottage for at least twenty years (1871-1891). Like the tall communications tower in the village today, the windmill was frequently struck by lightning. One of Rainbird's daughters had a lucky escape one day when lightning 'struck the sail, and then entered the roof, passed downwards through each floor of the building, and passed out just above the doorway, causing a rent in the brickwork.' It was reported that the miller's daughter was sitting at the door of Mill Cottage and experienced a serious shock.[16]

The last occupants of the mill from around 1899 were William Purkis and his wife, Eliza. The windmill was a popular subject for photographers and William and Eliza often posed for them in front of the windmill. (Figs. 5 and 78) The windmill was demolished in, or shortly before, 1920. One source suggests that during the First World War the Zeppelins used the windmill as a navigation aid and so it was demolished, however, an inhabitant of that time made no suggestion of this in his recollections about the village. The windmill appears on the 1920 Ordnance Survey Map, but is missing from a 1920 map of the Kelvedon Hall estate. Whenever it was demolished, its demolition was probably the outcome of an economic decision as opposed to a military decision.

Fig. 5. William and Eliza Purkis (standing).

Fig. 6. Mill Villas behind Mill Cottage.

Mill Villas [2]

Next to Mill Cottage was Mill Villas; a pair of semi-detached, red-brick and tiled houses, owned by the Kelvedon Hall estate. Built in the first decade of the twentieth century, each house had a sitting room, kitchen, pantry-larder and three bedrooms, with an outside wash-house and earth closet.[18] An early occupant was the village policeman, Constable Edward Barrett. They are now called Mill Villa and Black Feather.

Mushroom Hall [3] *d.*

Fig. 7 Mushroom Hall viewed from Eagle Lane.

The white gate in Fig.6 led to a property called Mushroom Hall (also called the Roundhouse, and later The Bungalow). It was built around 1800 to replace two cottages which had been burnt down. A single storey building built in the 'picturesque style', in 1893 the property included 'a stable, chaise-house, outbuildings, large gardens, and 3 acres of meadow land nearby'.[19]

For over 60 years the house was owned by the Keating family who lived in The Keatings, (later called The Chase [27]). They let the house to middle-class tenants and those of independent means. These included John Squire, a retired farmer; the unmarried Newenham sisters; and two retired butlers.

The first of these former butlers was James Clarkson who had been butler to John Francis Wright of Kelvedon Hall [51] for over 30 years. His wife, Susanna, had been the housekeeper. After Wright's death in 1865, they moved into Mushroom Hall. Clarkson continued to be employed on the estate as an under land-steward. Surprisingly, he was quite well-off for a former servant. He owned some properties situated opposite Mushroom Hall: the Guardsman [19] and four cottages [18 and 20]. After Clarkson came the second retired butler, William Gould. He had acted as butler to John Royds of Brizes [28] for at least fifteen years. Upon his retirement, he moved into Mushroom Hall with his wife, Francis. In 1893 he purchased the house from the executors of the estate of the last member of the Keating family. During his retirement, Gould was a parish councillor for a several years.

Poor's Cottages [4] *d.*

Fig. 8. Poor's Cottages viewed from Eagle Lane.

Leaving Mushroom Hall and returning to the Ongar Road, nearby is Eagle Lane. This was one of the trackways across the common and led to Stondon Massey and Blackmore. After enclosure of the common, hedges and oak trees were planted on either side of the lane.

A short distance down Eagle Lane on the left stood the property known as Poor's Cottages. Here lived the poorest families in Kelvedon Hatch. Owned by 'the unknown donor's charity' - better known as Poor's Charity - it was administered by the Overseers of the Kelvedon Poor (later called the Parochial Trustees); in effect the rector and a number of parish residents. By 1900, two other parish charities had been added (these had earlier been invested in stock which generated an annual return of dividends). All three were now administered as one charity.

The early history of the unknown donor's charity is unclear as many of the documents contradict each other and some are missing, but the situation by 1834 was that there were four adjoining cottages let on a weekly basis to the poor of the parish. Adjoining them was an area of land known as Poor's Field. This was part of the former common and had been provided in 1816 by the lord of the manor to the trustees of the charity. It was held copyhold of the manor. As mentioned earlier, a further piece of land was added to this field in 1831. The whole of the charity now consisted of 6 acres, and Poor's Field was rented out to the tenant farmer of Hatch Farm [13] for agriculture.

The cottages were described as a 'timber-framed T-shaped block, partly plastered and partly weather-boarded. There are gabled dormers in the tiled roof.'[20] The charity struggled to maintain the property. It was re-thatched in 1843, and in 1891, £50 was spent on improvements, but five years later, it was described as dilapidated. Again renovations were undertaken. Its brick floor was replaced by deal planks and the outside was repainted and tarred. Even wallpaper was allowed in two of the cottages!

According to the 1871 census, three families lived in these small cottages: twelve adults and seventeen children. It must have been very noisy inside as the walls were only constructed of wattle and daub. The residents of the cottages were required to have good moral standards. The overseers debated for some time over whether one labourer, George Sarling, should be required to quit because of non-payment of rent and the immoral life of his daughter: she was unmarried and had become pregnant. He was fortunate that she married soon after and that he managed to find the rent money.

After the cost of maintenance of the cottages had been deducted, the total income from the rent of the cottages and Poor's Field, and the dividends from investments, was distributed every January among the needy in the village. This was commonly known as 'Poor's Money'. Only certain people were eligible. It depended on their current income, the ages of their children, and their morals: no unwedded mothers; immoral characters; or those with criminal convictions in the previous year, including drunkenness. The pay-out took take place in the Eagle Inn [24], but this was later changed to the village school when it was realised that some of the distribution was immediately passing over the bar. In 1902, 106 villagers received five shillings a head.[21]

In the 1900s it was suggested that Poor's Field should be used for the building of cottages for the poor, but fortunately for the present-day villagers, this did not go ahead. Poor's Field is now the site of the village hall, children's play area, tennis courts and football pitch.

Cottages [5]

Returning to the windmill and then north up Mill Lane, on the right is a cottage. Now one dwelling called The Cottage, it was originally a pair of semi-detached cottages covered in black weather-boarding. Built in the early-nineteenth century, each cottage consisted of four rooms: two up, two down. This was a freehold property and let to agricultural workers. In 1891, five adults and nine children lived in these two small cottages. One of them was the Fitch family, and in particular, John Page Fitch whose recollections are used as a source of information for this book.

Fig. 9. Cottage in Mill Lane.
The former common land in front of the cottage has now been turned to agriculture.

Fig. 10. Mill Lane looking towards the windmill and the cottage.

Coppice Cottage [6] *d.*

Continuing north up Mill Lane we reach the junction with School Road. Opposite is a trackway once known as Coppice Gate. Over to the right is a housing development called The Coppice. Here stood Coppice Cottage. Coppice Cottage was originally two adjoining cottages (Fig. 11). Following alterations towards the end of the nineteenth century, it became one cottage consisting of two sitting rooms, a kitchen and three bedrooms.[22] (Fig. 12) The property of the Kelvedon Hall estate, it was occupied in the main by agricultural workers. The lady in the picture (Fig. 12) is Mary Ann Williamson. Her husband, John, was employed as a carpenter.

The underlying geology of the old common land meant that obtaining fresh water was a problem for the commoners. There were a number of private wells and pumps in the village, but they were not accessible to all the commoners. A well had been dug at the Poor's Cottages and there were complaints by the trustees that other commoners were using this resource; while at the Church House [14], it was found that a well of over 40 feet deep would be required. The water source usually used by the commoners was a spring which lay behind Coppice Cottage in Coppice Woods, almost one hundred yards down a track and then a steep path. None of the commoners looked forward to the toil of collecting the day's supply of drinking water.

In 1902, as part of the King Edward's coronation celebrations, it was decided that subscriptions would be raised to purchase and build a pump at the top of the Coppice, and to build a wall around the spring to stop contamination. The money raising was successful and pipes were installed leading from the spring to the pump. One parishioner regarded it as 'one of the greatest blessings that this Parish had at that time and for a very long time',[23] although others complained that the pump was hard to operate.

In Poles Wood, a few hundred yards to the north of Coppice Cottage, stood a shooting range used by the Essex Volunteer Rifle Corps. Founded in 1859, this was one of the many county volunteer corps created by a government which was in fear of an invasion by the French. The nearest unit was based at Chipping Ongar: the 18th (Ongar) Volunteer Corps. Members were subject to military discipline, received military training, and could be called upon in the event of an invasion or rebellion. To aid their training, a firing range was constructed on land owned by Kelvedon Hall [51] and Great Myles [58]. The firing points were in neighbouring Stondon Massey while the butts were in Poles Wood. Apart from using it for training, corps members also took part in a monthly shooting contest which became a popular event at which many parishioners came to spectate. Several years later, a government review of the Volunteer Rifle Corps led to the amalgamation of many units and the range ceased to be used.[24]

Fig. 11. Coppice Cottage before conversion.

Fig. 12. Coppice Cottage after conversion. Photograph c..1906

Bungalows [7] *d.*

Next to Coppice Cottage were two small bungalows built in the first decade of the 1900s. Nothing else is known about them. In 1911, one was occupied by Ernest Roe and his family. Roe was a coachman, so he probably worked either at Brizes or Kelvedon Hall. The other was the home of Elizabeth Harris, a widower, and her two children.

Woodlands [8]

On the other side of Coppice Gate is the property now known as Woodlands. Here once stood three terraced cottages occupied by agricultural workers. The cottages dated from at least the 1740s, probably much earlier, and the plot included a large pasture field to the rear. In 1883 the cottages were sold to a William Wilson, of whom nothing else is known. He demolished them and in their place built the present house.[25, 26]

In 1889 the house was purchased by William Dutton for the sum of £600. Dutton had a career in the post office. Starting off as a letter carrier in London in 1855, by 1871 he was a letter sorter living in Forest Gate, and when he moved to Kelvedon Hatch he had worked his way up to the position of overseer. This was to be his last move; in 1901 he retired from the Post Office. Dutton became an important and well respected member of the community and served on the parish council. Several of Dutton's children also chose the post office as a career, including his daughter, Alice, who became the sub-postmistress at Kelvedon Hatch. We shall read a little more about them when we come to the post office [16] which William Dutton built. Dutton sold the house in 1908 to Edwin Allan Patterson, an engineer, for £530. It is not known why Dutton sold this house at such a substantial loss. After settling in, Patterson also served on the parish council.

Army Huts [9]

Moving along School Road (which, incidentally, was only a footpath until the parish vestry decided to build the road in 1850), on the right is a plot of land which includes Greenways, a converted former army hut from the First World War. At the time of writing this book this plot of land is undergoing redevelopment.

This now provides the opportunity to look at how the people of Kelvedon Hatch found themselves at the front line of Britain's land and air defences during World War One. After the declaration of war against Germany in August 1914, there was a great fear that the Germans would invade England. To counter this threat and protect London, a line of trenches was dug across Essex. Locally, they ran through Mountnessing, Doddinghurst, Stondon Massey, Ongar and Shelley. Two miles behind these trenches, the people of Kelvedon Hatch were called upon to quarter some of the hundreds of army personnel involved in this massive undertaking. In December 1914, quarters for 250 troops had to found; and in May 1915, 60 men of the Royal Warwickshire Regiment were quartered in the parish. It must have been interesting to listen to some of the conversations involving the Essex dialect and the Coventry and Birmingham dialects. Two weeks later it would even be more confusing with the arrival of the Welsh and the Monmouthshire Regiment whose number included many former miners who were bringing their expertise to the digging.[27]

As the fear of invasion subsided, quartering was no longer required; besides, the authorities found that quartering adversely affected the troops' discipline. The next time scores of troops were seen in the parish was towards the end of the war when food was rationed. Parishioners would have seen troops working in the fields helping with food production and working parties of German prisoners of war would have been a regular sight.

The greatest effect on the parishioners, however, was from the aerial war against the German Zeppelins. On the north side of this plot of land stood a machine gun (later replaced by a higher calibre gun) and a searchlight. These were part of London's air defences. Every night army crews used the searchlight to scan the skies looking for Zeppelins making their way to and from London. Later, searchlights were also placed in the grounds of Brizes [28] and in a field opposite the Rectory [60]. The guns and searchlights played a role in the shooting down of Zeppelin L33 on 23 September 1916, L31 on 1 October 1916, as well as shooting at L15 on 13 October 1915, and engaging other airships.[28] On the night of 31 March 1916, thirteen bombs were dropped by a Zeppelin over Blackmore and Stondon Massey causing violent shakings of windows. Fortunately there were no casualties. At the time it was thought that firing from the Kelvedon Common gun had prompted the Zeppelin's captain to drop the bombs as a self-defence measure.

The roar of the Zeppelin engines, gunfire and explosions could be heard across the countryside. A woman living in a neighbouring parish wrote in her diary: 'an air-craft raid took place on the night of April 2, and from the Rectory we could plainly hear the engines of a Zeppelin airship, and the frequent discharges of the machine gun at Kelvedon Hatch which was responded to by others posted at different points in the surrounding country.'[29] Another observer in nearby Stondon Massey described the cacophony of sounds from frightened animals and birds which followed gunfire and explosions: 'I have never heard such a harmony: bullocks, cows, calves, lambs, sheep, horse, dogs, fowls, rooks and pheasants: all might be heard calling in the night: all terrified and wondering what was the cause of the sudden clash into the silence'.[30]

The strategic importance of the Kelvedon Hatch battery was emphasised when William Weal found himself in front of the magistrates' court after breaking the blackout regulations by lighting a fire on his Common Gardens' allotment which lay across the road from the battery. He was fined 5s.[31]

As well as a gun and searchlight, here could be found storage sheds and ammunition handling facilities, and army huts used as the crew's quarters. Immediately after the war, two of the huts were converted into a dwelling of four and two rooms, respectively.[32] This property is now called Greenways.

In common with hundreds of other parishes, in 1920 the parish council erected a war memorial to the memory of those who had fallen in the war. The war memorial is currently sited further along School Road on the junction with Ongar Road. This is its latest location. It was originally sited 200 yards to the south on the west side of Ongar Road (Fig. 35), but was moved because of the increasing traffic on the Ongar Road. These are the names of those who died in the First World War and which appear on the memorial (in date order).

> Private John King, 13th Battalion, Essex Regiment. Killed in action on 13 November 1916 in France. Born in Kelvedon Hatch in 1890, he was the son of George and Sarah King. A single man, he lived in the family home at Caton's Cottages [21]. He worked as a bricklayers' labourer.
>
> Private Bertie Cowling, 6th Battalion, Leicester Regiment. Killed in action on 14 November 1916 in France. Born in Navestock, c.1883, before the war he lived in Navestock and Stapleford Tawney. It appears he married a woman named Elizabeth and moved into one of the cottages in The Avenue [32], but because there is a gap in the records, it is not possible to supply the full details.
>
> Lieutenant-Colonel Sidney Goss Mullock, Essex Regiment. Killed in action on 12 April 1917 in France. Aged 36 and originally from Wales, he was married with two children. He lived at The Chase [27].
>
> Private Sidney Metson, 1st Battalion, Royal Irish Fusiliers. Killed in action on 23 November 1917 in France. Born in Great Leighs in 1897 to Walter and Julia Metson, by 1916 the family had moved to Beacon Hill Cottages [47].
>
> Lieutenant John Iltid Royds, London Regiment (Artists' Rifles) 1st/28th Battalion. Killed in action on 22 March 1918 in France. He was single, aged 42, he was the second son of Charles and Ada Royds of Brizes [28]. He appears in the census returns twice under Brizes [1901 and 1911], so this may have been his permanent home.

The Artists' Rifles was a corps consisting of painters, sculptors, engravers, musicians, architects and actors. In his case, Royds was an artist, although examples of his work have not been found.

Private Reginald Hunt, Army Service Corps Motor Transport. Died of his wounds in the 1st Southern General Hospital, Edgbaston, Birmingham, on 6 November 1918. Aged 27 at the time of his death, Hunt was born in Worcestershire. By the time of the 1911 census he was employed as a chauffeur. It may well be that his job brought him to Kelvedon Hatch. In 1915, he met and married Margaret Williamson who lived at Coppice Cottage with her parents [6]. This then became his home for his short married life. Margaret remarried in 1921.

School and School House [10]

Further along School Road is the school. Prior to the building of the school in 1879, there was no government or county funding for schools and money had to be gathered by means of voluntary subscriptions. The parish rectors took on the task of trying to educate the parishioners. Various parliamentary reports provide sketchy information on the education being provided. In 1819, it was reported there were two day schools: 'one supported by a lady, and the other by the rector's wife, containing together about 40 children'. It was found that 'the poor are supplied with books from the Society for Promoting Christian knowledge.'[33] Fourteen years later there was 'one Day School and Sunday School, at which 30 females attend daily, with the addition of from 10 to 20 males on Sundays; this school is supported by voluntary contributions'.[34]

By 1839, the Revd John Bannister, rector of Kelvedon Hatch [60], had rented a house for use as a school. Located just over the parish boundary in Doddinghurst in what is now the road named Finchingfields [64], it served both parishes. The school consisted of two large rooms, while the common opposite served as a playground.[35] The house was also the home of the teacher: William Nutt in 1841, and William John Macartney in 1851. A report of 1839 reveals that boys were also attending this day school and the rector even supplied clothing for the pupils. The boys were given 'smocks, stockings, hats, and handkerchiefs', while the girls had complete sets of clothing.[36] No fees were involved, unless the parents wished their children to learn how to write, then it cost 3d a week.

In 1848, the Committee on Education reported that 'the attendance is irregular and not punctual. The reading very defective in the girls' school; rather better in the boys' school. Some children show intelligence and knowledge of Scripture.'[37] Four years later it was found that the 'building [was] fair...furniture, apparatus, discipline, instruction very moderate'.[38]

This school appears to have closed by the 1860s, and a later report reveals that the next school was small with no permanent teacher or accommodation. It was described as a 'dame school' and was funded by the then rector, the Revd Samuel Slocock. Some parish schools acquired this name because they were often run by elderly spinsters or widows. This was certainly the case in Kelvedon Hatch. In 1871, the schoolmistress was Annie Noakes, a widower, who had 18 scholars. At the time she was living at Old Crown [42]; perhaps this is where the school was located. She may have been assisted by two young people who lived in the village: Stephen Thomas, aged 15, who was described as a pupil teacher, and Emily Ffitch, aged 18, described as a schoolmistress.

Fig. 13. The new school with the schoolmaster's house at the far end.

In 1875, under the power vested by the Education Act of 1870, a school board was created in the parish to undertake the permanent establishment of a school. The board members were the Revd Samuel Slocock, chairman and treasurer [60]; Edward Carington Wright, lord of the manor and of Kelvedon Hall [51]; James French, a farmer [56]; Robert John French, a farmer [48]; and Henry Knightbridge, a butcher [35].[39] It is interesting to note that Carington Wright, a Roman Catholic, became involved in the creation of the school. Elections for subsequent board members were held every three years.

A field was purchased to the north of the former common land and building of the school commenced in 1878. The bad weather of that winter played havoc with its construction and it was not until the following November that it was finished. It cost £850 to build (excluding the land) and could accommodate 80 children.[40] A schoolmaster's house was built attached to the school. Later alterations to the school included an extension, the addition of cloakrooms, and separate entrances for boys and girls.

The first schoolmaster was Henry Thomas Cawdron, assisted by his daughter, Francis. Cawdron had been a schoolmaster for over 30 years. His previous school had been at Terling, Essex, and the move to Kelvedon Hatch may have been prompted by the death of his wife in 1877. The first page of the school log book for the 28 November 1879 records the first day:

> 'On Monday last the handsome and commodious school buildings lately erected in this parish of Kelvedon Hatch were opened for the reception of children. Previously the only means the parish had been able to furnish for their accommodation and instruction had been a cottage and an elderly dame to teach. As might be naturally expected, the children were found by the new teachers to be totally unacquainted with the forms of discipline now required in the management of schools; and, before the formation of constituted authority, had attended only as their parents thought fit to send them …'[41]

As Cawdron wrote in these opening words, discipline would be an immediate challenge. Many of the children had not attended school before. The school log book contains his many observations on the children and his frustration with their behaviour: 'stupid and sullen over their sums'; 'stubbornness is a characteristic'; 'it is hoped that the children are making progress, though many are dull and some very wilful and stubborn'; and 'another disgusting offence in the shape of filthy writing was found'.

He also had confrontations with parents after he had administered corporal punishment to their children. On one occasion using a '12 inch stick weighing no more than one-third of ounce', he had punished one of the pupils, William Enever. His father threatened to 'take the law in his own hands'. In another incident, Cawdron stopped Thomas King assaulting a girl. He later wrote that, 'when the teacher went to protect her, the Commoners set upon him like a pack of wolves'. Cawdron went on to observe that 'intimidation is the game they are playing at, which the teacher intends shall be a losing one to them'.

He also wrote of his frustration with parents who stopped their children from attending the school as they were needed to help out with field work and tasks at home. Indeed, all the teachers found that school attendance clashed with the need for a family to have additional income, no matter how small. Cawdron was also the area attendance officer. On several occasions he took parents before the magistrates' court at Ongar where they were fined for keeping their children away from school. Before schooling became free there were also problems with parents not having the money to pay for their child's education. Costing two pence a week, many parents relied on the Poor's Money annual pay-out to help pay the fees.

Cawdron received an adverse report from the School Inspectors in 1883 for which he laid the blame on the school board for not supporting him. This came to a head in April 1884 when Cawdron resigned. His final words in the school log again imply criticism of the school board's failure to support him.

After a short period when there was an unknown master, in October 1884, Charles White became schoolmaster. He was assisted by his wife, Marion. White had started his teaching career in Bethnal Green in London's East End, so moving to a school in the country must have been a very different teaching experience for him. White was later joined by some teaching assistants: Miss Maling and Miss Randall; and after they left, by Alice Dutton, of Woodlands [8], who worked as assistant school mistress until she left to take over the post office [16] in 1899.

White worked hard to improve discipline, and he reported that attendance had greatly improved. His log book entries are rather shorter than his predecessor's. He made brief comments on lesson plans, inspections and the absence of pupils due to sickness. Although the health of children slowly improved during the Victorian period, the log book shows that there were still many childhood diseases which could be fatal. On 7 May 1886, he wrote: 'a little boy named William King died this week from diphtheria, after a few days' illness'. There were also numerous reports of measles, mumps, ringworm, scarlet fever, smallpox and typhoid fever. On occasions, outbreaks of some diseases meant the temporary closure of the entire school.

White became an important member of the community. He was an avid musician, and became the organist and choir master at the church. He organised social functions at the school and helped raise money for the new church. He was also a keen cyclist. His death in 1908, at the age of 50, was a shock to the community. It was reported that his widow received hundreds of letters of condolence. After the death of her husband, Marion White remained at the school as school mistress and assistant to the new school master, William Tilley, a single man. Her daughter, Florence, also assisted as a teacher.

The convenient location of the school meant that it became an important venue for parish meetings and social events, particularly during the last decade of the nineteenth century. It was seen as the sober alternative to holding meetings in public houses. The parish magazine carried news of these events. Here are just some of the events held in the schoolroom between the years 1893 and 1898.[42]

Figs. 14 and 15 Charles and Marion White with their pupils, c.1893. Note the post boy in his uniform, and the out-grown 'Sunday best' of the boy (above).

Church events included church services, a Sunday school, and the Church of England Temperance Society meetings. The temperance movement was strongly supported by the middle class in Kelvedon Hatch, and they urged the working man to avoid the temptation of drink and to stop visiting public houses. For the children there was the 'Band of Hope', established to teach them about the evils of drink. One of their meetings included a lecture on the effects of drink on the brain, lungs and heart. Other church events included rummage sales to raise money towards the building of the new church; a lecture on keeping homes healthy; and a Sunday school treat of tea and cakes. Other parish events included a lecture on Canada - with the aid of a magic lantern. The village soiree and dance was very popular: two people from each house in the parish were invited and they were supplied with tea, cakes, buns, and coffee, while a small orchestra provided the music. There were also shows by singers, a ventriloquist, and a conjurer.

The annual pay out of Poor's Charity and payments for use of the Common Gardens, both formerly in the Eagle Inn, now took place in the schoolroom. The attendees of the latter were provided with tea, cakes, and tobacco, and were entertained with songs. In 1897, the Queen's diamond jubilee celebrations took place in the field to the rear of the school. The parishioners were entertained by a conjurer, and there were swings, roundabouts, a coconut shy, races for adults and children; music and dancing; with the day ending with fireworks. In 1894, the Local Government Act created Parish Councils which took responsibility for parish administration away from the parish vestry system. From then onwards Parish Council meetings were held in the schoolroom.

After the establishment of the Church House [14] and changes to the management of the school by the new County Council, with the exception of parish council meetings, the school was no longer used for meetings and parish events.

Cottages [11] *d.*

Leaving the school and continuing along School Road to the junction with the Ongar Road, on the right are the modern houses of Thatch Cottage and Kames House. The war memorial stands between them.

The area of land on which these two modern houses now stand was once the site of the parish poorhouse. Before 1834, the parish poor were the responsibility of each individual parish. Parish administration was conducted through the parish vestry system. Members of the parish vestry (so called because it normally met in the church vestry), were residents of the parish, normally the rector, landowners, farmers and rate-paying tradesmen. From their number were appointed two churchwardens, two road surveyors, two or three constables, two overseers and two assessors. The roles of the surveyors and constables will be described later.

The assessor's task was to assess the value of properties in the parish and set a poor rate which house owners had to pay. For example, in 1836 it was set at four shillings in the pound. This money was then used by the overseers to alleviate the suffering of the poor and infirm in the parish. They also maintained a poorhouse for the old and the destitute. Unfortunately, no description of the poorhouse survives, but judging by its size on the tithe map, it was probably only of two or three rooms. Some of the overseers' accounts, however, do survive from this time. These reveal that weekly disbursements were made to those out of work, ill, or with young babies. These disbursements were in cash, or as items such as clothing, coal, or bread. In the year 1833, £266 was spent by the overseers. The parish even paid to send George Pizney, a young boy, to join the navy.[43]

Following the introduction of a new Poor Law in 1834, Kelvedon Hatch was joined with a number of surrounding parishes in the newly created Ongar Poor Law Union. Money from the parish poor rate now went to the Ongar Poor Law Union which maintained the newly built workhouse in Stanford Rivers. The new Poor Law was intended to bring to an end out-relief for the able bodied. They could only obtain relief in the workhouse. But it transpired that the vast majority of people admitted to the workhouse were the old and infirm, orphans, unmarried mothers, and the physically or mentally ill.

As the parish poorhouse was no longer required, the parish sold the poorhouse and the land. The poorhouse was demolished and replaced by four terraced cottages of timber and thatch with two rooms in each.[44] Living in one of these two-roomed cottages for over 50 years were William Jarvis and his wife, Mary. Working most of his life on the land as a farm labourer, by the time Jarvis was in his late 60s he was unable to manage hard work in the fields and so he looked after the horses on one of the farms. At the beginning of the twentieth century, these four cottages were converted into one cottage which became known as Thatch Cottage.

Weal's Cottages [12] d.

Also built on the same plot of land were three brick-built terraced cottages with four rooms in each cottage.[45] These became known as Weal's Cottages. They gained their name from one of their occupants in the second half of the century: the Weal family (also spelt Wheal in some records). William Weal was a hay and coal carter, and by 1890 he owned at least four carts. As well as carting hay, he helped people move home, transport goods, and conveyed people to and from the railway stations at

Fig. 16. Weal's Cottages (left), Cottages (later Thatch Cottage) (right).
The advertisement on the side of the waggon reads: 'W. Weal, carman and contractor, Kelvedon Hatch, goods carefully removed'.

Fig. 17. The same view taken a few years later.
The hut in the middle (which was hidden in the first photograph) carries an advertisement for Raleigh. Presumably, Weal now also repaired cycles. The building on the right is the new post office [16]

Brentwood and Ongar. He was particularly busy when there were special outings organised in the parish. On the occasion of a church choir outing to London, he took them to Brentwood Station first thing in the morning. From there, the choir went on to visit St Paul's Cathedral, the Egyptian Hall, and then took a boat to Greenwich. Upon their return to Brentwood they were again transported by Weal. On the day of the parish excursion to Southend, he was even busier: 125 villagers took the trip. This was the most successful parish outing; the least successful trip was to London, only fourteen took part.

Hatch Farm [13]

Fig. 18. Hatch Farm 1907.

Just after turning right into the Ongar Road is Hatch Farm. Built in the sixteenth century with later alterations, it was part of the Kelvedon Hall estate. The house replaced an earlier medieval house. In 1920 it was described as having a 'square hall, dining room, drawing room, five bedrooms, kitchen, scullery, dairy, wash-house, earth closet, and a range of farm buildings'.[46] At varying times, the farm consisted of between 80 and 110 acres, and during the nineteenth century it was occupied by many different tenant farmers. In front of the farm and fed by a spring, was a large pond which made it a convenient spot for passing carters and drovers to stop and water their animals [Fig. 18].

As this is the first of several farms on the tour, it will now be useful to look at the state of farming in Kelvedon Hatch and Essex during this period.

After a prosperous mid-nineteenth century, towards the end of the century, farming in Essex was a challenge for both farmers and landowners because of a wide-spread agricultural depression. Essex was mainly a corn growing district but there had been a succession of poor harvests and seasons of bad weather. In addition, cheap grain imports from America meant low prices at which the farmer could sell their produce. The heavy clays of Essex were found to be so unproductive that by 1894, 13% of Essex's arable farmland was abandoned and turned to rough pasture.[47] All these factors meant that many farmers were in financial difficulties. Farm buildings also deteriorated. Tenant farmers were unwilling to invest in their farms while they struggled to pay their rents. Landowners, meanwhile, found their incomes cut. Some abandoned the farms, while others tried to promote a change to different types of farming, but many older farmers were set in their ways. In Kelvedon Hatch, some of the farmers at Germains Farm [48] and Langford Bridge Farm [56] tried switching to pasture and cattle, but on the remaining farms, farmers struggled on with the primary crops of wheat, oats and barley, while in Doddinghurst, pea growing was found to be successful.

Fig. 19. After the fire at Hatch Farm 29 August 1909.

Meanwhile, the farmers still had everyday problems to deal with. Fire was an ever present risk, caused by an accident or by children playing with matches, or even deliberate arson. Arson was particularly prevalent in Victorian times when disgruntled labourers set fire to crops and ricks belonging to their employers or former employers. One such incidence of arson occurred in November 1899 at Hatch Farm when it was being farmed by James Newcombe of Beacon Hill Farm, Navestock. The fire was discovered in the farmyard by a neighbour, George Randall, the blacksmith [17]. He raised the alarm and the fire engine at Ongar was sent for. William Weal from Weal's Cottages [12], together with his sons, arrived to tackle the blaze. On the arrival of the fire brigade, the fire was extinguished. The loss amounted to three stacks of hay, one of straw and two of clover. Arson was suspected because there had been two other incidences in the previous week - one of them at Mushroom Hall [3] where a hay stack had been destroyed, and the other at the Eagle Inn [24].[48,49] There is no report of the culprit being found. Eight years later there was another fire involving ricks. But the worst fire was in August 1909 when it destroyed the barn, stables, tool-house and cow-house, causing damage valued at £500 (Fig. 19).[50]

Another example of the risky business of farming occurred in 1898 when the Newcombes suffered a family bereavement. William Newcombe, who helped his brother at Hatch Farm, was driven to a nervous breakdown by the results of a ferocious thunder and hailstorm which made its way across Essex on 24 June 1897, just as harvest-time was approaching. Within twenty minutes, hailstones said to be over 2 inches in diameter had flattened crops, reduced vegetables to pulp, destroyed orchards, and smashed over 500 panes of glass in the greenhouses at Brizes, and 400 at Kelvedon Hall. It was estimated that across the parish the cost of the damage amounted to £2000. The rector observed that, 'never in the memory of the oldest inhabitant has such a storm been known in the parish'.[51] After the storm William Newcombe went out to view the devastation in the fields and broke down exclaiming: 'We are ruined! We are ruined!' Soon after this his mental and medical condition rapidly deteriorated leading to his committal to the Essex County Lunatic Asylum where he died soon after.[52] Many farmers in Essex went bankrupt because of this storm. An appeal was launched, and a year later the Essex Storm Relief Committee distributed money to over 3,100 farmers, some individuals receiving over £400. [53]

Soon after the fire of 1899, James Newcombe stopped farming at Hatch Farm and it was taken over by George Randall, the son of the blacksmith who had discovered the fire. Randall had recently married Kathleen Cousens and they had two children: Ellen (Nessie) and Annie. The family did not stay at Hatch Farm for long. In 1906 they emigrated to Saskatchewan, Canada, where things did not go well for the family. By the time of the 1911 census, George had died, leaving Kathleen to bring up her family now consisting of five daughters.

By 1909, the land at Hatch Farm was being farmed by Isaiah Mugleston of Langford Bridge Farm [56].

Figs. 20 and 21. These photographs taken at Hatch Farm are believed to be that of Kathleen Randall and her daughters.

Part 2

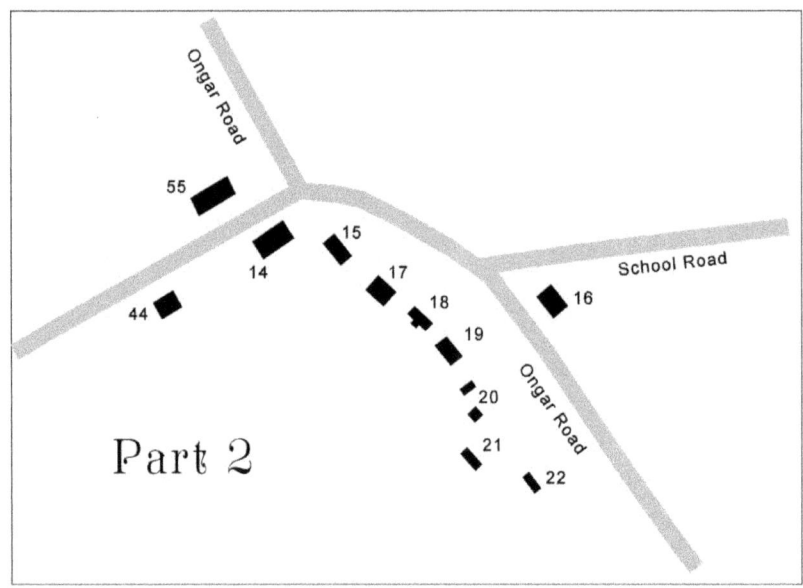

Fig. 22.

The Church [see 55]

Opposite Hatch Farm is St Nicholas' Church. Built in 1895, it replaced the parish church in the grounds of Kelvedon Hall. The story of both churches can be found at [54] and [55].

Ryansville / Church House [14]

Opposite the church is a property that was originally designed to be both a home and a post office. It then underwent several changes in use, but is now again the village's post office and general stores.

Sometime in the mid-1870s, Joseph Aloysius Ryan Rorke and his wife, Esther, moved to the parish and into the Guardsman [19] (as it was later called), and took over the running of the general store and post office. At first he appears to have been a little naive in business matters because he allowed a local farmer, George Littlechild of Pump House Farm [61], to run up the considerable debt of £33 by allowing him credit. The matter was eventually taken before the civil court and he recovered his money.[54]

In 1880, Rorke obtained a 99-year lease on a plot of land owned by the Brizes estate [28]. After obtaining a mortgage, he built himself a new house which he proudly called Ryansville. Rorke remained the sub-postmaster and

Fig. 23. Church House c.1905. Certainly an unusual design.

part of his new house became the post office. The property contained two bedrooms, a dressing room, two sitting rooms, kitchen and scullery, and an office for use as the post office.[55]

Naming the house after himself is consistent with a man with an ego. The same impression is given when one reads his letters and newspaper articles about him. He dabbled in local politics and often wrote to the newspapers correcting their articles or voicing his opinions. He also managed to upset his neighbours to the extent that one of them, Thomas Ratcliff, assaulted him.[56] In June 1896, Rorke resigned his position as sub-postmaster and later offered his house for sale.[57] The conveyancing documents reveal that he was particularly difficult with the new purchaser and drove a hard bargain. It is not known what prompted him to leave his home and job to move to West Ham for the position of a manager in a tinplate factory.

The use of the building then took an unusual change. A few years earlier in 1893, as well as raising funds for a new church, the rector and churchwardens had launched a parallel fund raising effort to raise money to build a working men's club and parish room. Their aim was to stop 'the temptation of drink' and to 'give brightness, warmth and recreation for the working men of the parish [and] to encourage: thrift, temperance, [and] domestic economy.'[58] As a temporary solution, the Revd Charles Royds [28] allowed part of Dodds Farm [44] to serve as a village club. The accommodation consisted of a reading room and a games room.[59] Access to these premises ceased in 1896.

The problem of finding suitable premises for a parish room was solved when Edward William Puxon, the father-in-law of the rector, the Revd David Wilkie Peregrine, purchased Ryansville from Rorke. He then let the property at a nominal rent for use as a club and parish room. After a number of changes to the building's interior, and now with the new name of Church House, it was opened on 7 December 1897.[60]

The working men's club was open from 6pm to 10pm every night of the week. Members paid 4 shillings for a year's membership. In the club there was a reading room with daily newspapers and a library of over 200 books; a games room; and a billiards and bagatelle room. There was also a committee room for church or parish business. The entrance hall doubled as a public coffee tavern - a popular stopping-off point for week-end cyclists. As well as offering an alternative to the public house and providing self-education, it was hoped that thrift would be encouraged. There was a penny bank, a coal club, a boot club and a clothing club. Supervising the premises and its members were two live-in caretakers: Golden Williams and his wife, Margaret. Williams was also the verger and sexton at the church.[61]

A boys' club was also held here three times a week, but as to what the activities were, it is not recorded. Apart from one letter, the voices of the young people of the parish are silent in the records. The one surviving letter suggests that despite being surrounded by countryside, there seems to have been no area for the youngsters to play football. This unknown youth appealed for help in the parish magazine:

'Sir, Will anyone help us boys?

We have nowhere to play out of school hours - not even the playground - except the roads. Here we get into trouble by doing things we ought not to, so people call us a rough and rude lot. Is it fair? Do we boys of Keldon Parish have even a chance given us of doing any better? Do, someone, lend us a field to play in; we should love to have a game of cricket and rounders. Then people would begin to say what a nice behaved lot those Keldon Lads are.

Yours obediently,

Young Keldon'[62]

Between the Church Room and Dodds Farm [44] there is a field. This now became the venue for open-air events such as coronation celebrations, annual fetes, and cricket and football matches. The first mention of an official Kelvedon Hatch football team is from 1918, although it is believed there was a team before then. Cricket clubs for both men and boys were established upon the opening of the Church Room and they used it as their club room. This was not the first cricket club in the parish. The previous rector, Revd Slocock, was a keen cricketer; in his younger days he had played for Berkshire. During his time in the parish, he organised a cricket team under the name of Kelvedon Hatch, but it was not representative of the parish, most of its members were former university friends of Slocock. A cricket team with a little more representative selection of parishioners was organised by the local gentry in the 1850s and 60s. John Francis Wright of Kelvedon Hall [51] and Countess Waldegrave of nearby Dubrook Hall arranged an annual cricket match which was played on the Navestock cricket ground. Each team was made up of people who worked on their estates or were connected with the estates: farmers, servants and tradesmen. Their numbers were bolstered by friends of the hosts. Each match became a social event with a band laid on and a meal supplied after the match. These matches stopped after the death of Wright. It was not until 1898 that there was a cricket club which truly contained a cross-section of all the parishioners.

Despite all the optimism, the parish club failed. By 1902, the accounts showed that the club was running at a loss. It was decided that a smaller premises would have to be found. In the meantime, the Church House became the curate's residence, and by 1911, it was let out to Edward Hardingham, a retired bank accountant.

Wesleyan Chapel / Parish Room [15] *d.*

The solution to the problem of the finances, or so it was thought at the time, was the purchase in 1907 of the former Wesleyan chapel which stood next door. The Wesleyan chapel had been unused for some years when the current rector, the Revd Laurence Tuttiett, suggested that it would be suitable for the new parish room. Two residents, Charles Royds of Brizes [28] and John Algernon Jones of Kelvedon Hall [51], loaned the money for the purchase of the freehold of the property and for the building's renovation.[63] It was their intention that it should be an asset for the entire parish, but this did not go to plan. It seems the legal documentation was too vague as to who owned the property and how it was to be used. The new rector in 1908, the Revd William Mavor, viewed it as a church asset and began to limit the use of the room to mainly church functions and the 'promotion of church work'.[64] His high-handed approach caused a great deal of upset in the parish. The parish council minutes reveal the frustrations of the parish councillors at their inability to use the room as an asset for all the community. 'Is it a church room or a parish room?' was an often asked question. The dispute rumbled on for years and there are even references to it in 1930 when the room was sold by Mavor.

The origins of this chapel lay in the open-air services held near the windmill by the Wesleyan Methodists in the 1870s. These services were well attended. On 22 April 1877, over 300 labourers and their families attended one service.[65] As these were open-air services, inclement weather was obviously a problem. It was resolved by the congregation that a chapel should be built. The following year, John Royds of Brizes [28] permitted the purchase of a lease on a small plot of land for the building of a chapel. Built of timber on a brick-work basement and lined throughout with match boarding, it was described as 'comfortably seated' and lit by a large chandelier suspended from the roof.[66] It was designed to hold 200 people.

These open-air services and the building of the dissenting chapel coincided with a decade of unrest and agitation by agricultural workers. In 1872, the Agricultural Labourers Union was established by Joseph Arch, an agricultural worker and Primitive Methodist preacher from Warwickshire. During its most active time, local union representatives recruited members, and helped them demand better wages and working conditions from the farmers and landowners.

Examples of how this affected those living in Kelvedon Hatch are few because most of the newspapers did not report these labour disputes. But there are some which are of interest. Between the years 1872 and 1877, the district president of union, John Killingback, held meetings on Navestock Heath which were attended by hundreds of labourers from the surrounding parishes. Meanwhile, the union canvassed for new members in the parish. At one meeting in a Doddinghurst beer house (possibly the Shepherd [71]), seventeen Kelvedon Hatch and Doddinghurst labourers were enrolled.[67] On the same night as this meeting, a barley straw stack was set alight near the Rectory [60]. A coincidence? No culprit was ever found.

Rural society was also changing because of the unrest. For 34 years there had been a Labourers' Friend Society based at Ongar. Administered by churchmen, landowners and farmers, its aim was to help the agricultural labourer. The names of many Kelvedon Hatch farm workers appear in articles referring to the society. In 1876, the committee recognised that the 'Society has ceased to be either sufficiently appreciated by or sufficiently useful to those whom it was intended to benefit...and that indifference has shown to it of late years by the labourers themselves',[68] The society was then wound-up. Finally, John Royds of Brizes regularly held an annual harvest home festival when up to 50 of his employees sat down with their employer and enjoyed a meal of beef, mutton, vegetables, and pudding, washed down with a 'foaming tankard' of beer. Reports of this cease after 1871.[69]

The activities and membership of Agricultural Labourers Union declined in the late 1870s. With the help of the Union, many of its former members left the country to seek a better life in the colonies. Its legacy was a fundamental change in the once paternal relationship which existed between landowners, farmers and their employees. Meanwhile, the Wesleyan Chapel continued its services until a declining congregation meant its final closure.

Fig. 24. A religious meeting near Coppice Cottage. A fine weather alternative to the church or parish room.

This event for children was held in a tent somewhere near to Coppice Cottage [6] around 1908-10. It could have been a Sunday school, or a children's Band of Hope meeting, or a service organised by a nonconformist mission.

Post Office [16]

After the resignation of Rorke, and the loss of a building in which to house the post office, a temporary corrugated iron hut was erected near the former chapel on land belonging to the Brizes estate. The exact location is not known.

The new sub-postmaster, Frederick Henry Brenes, commenced his duties in July 1896.[70] It is not known if Brenes appears in Fig. 25. Brenes lived in Great Warley, but moved into Dodds Farm [44] upon his appointment. Brenes was a keen bee keeper and member of the Essex Bee Keepers Association. He was no stranger to Kelvedon Hatch. A few years earlier at the church fete, he was due to give an exhibition on beekeeping. He had brought his bees with him, but his bee tent in which he was to exhibit them was taken in error by the delivery cart driver to Kelvedon instead of Kelvedon Hatch. This confusion over the names still occurs today. Brenes died in 1899 of typhoid – just 41 years old.

Fig. 25. The temporary post office.

After Brenes' death, Alice Dutton, whom we first met at Woodlands [8] and then the School [10], became the new sub-postmistress for Kelvedon Hatch. She would also have a new home for the post office within a few months. Her father, William Dutton, purchased a plot of land on the Ongar Road at its junction with School Road. Here he built a house and part of it became the new post office. The property was soon found to be too small for the family, so in 1905, it was extended.

The post office was a family business. Alice Dutton (right) was the sub-postmistress; William, her brother, was a sorting clerk; her other brother, Arthur, also helped out as assistant postmaster; while her cousin, Leonard, was a telegraph messenger and postman. Also, there were at least four or five other postmen and post boys. A large team was needed because the post office was open from 7am until 8pm with up to four collections  and deliveries, six days a week. Alice Dutton remained the sub-postmistress for almost 35 years. The former post office is now two private houses.

Above: Fig. 26. Alice Dutton.

Right: Figs. 27-29. The new post office became a popular subject for postcard photographers.

Red House [17]

Fig. 30. Red House.

The girl in the picture is Ellen (Nessie) Randall, mentioned under Hatch Farm [13].

Returning to the west side of the Ongar Road and to the property known as the Red House. This was the blacksmith's. The present house was built c.1845 and was owned by the Kelvedon Hall estate. In 1920 it was described as: 'red brick, slate roof, with a hall, sitting room, kitchen, back kitchen, dairy and four bedrooms'.[71] To one side of the property was the smithy, a workshop and storage sheds.[72] The Red House replaced an earlier cottage and smithy on this site. The tithe map also shows a building immediately in front of this earlier cottage. It also appears on Chapman and Andre map of 1777 (Fig. 2). Unfortunately, it has not been possible to find any further information about it. It was demolished before 1873.

For almost 40 years, the Brown family worked here as blacksmiths and wheelwrights, as well as looking after the mill for a time. Thomas Brown moved to the parish around 1848. He had three sons who also became blacksmiths, and when Thomas died, his son Edward took over the business assisted by his brother, Harry. The Browns left in the 1880s, and the Red House became the home of George Randall and his family. Like the Browns, theirs was a family business. His sons, Edward and George, were also blacksmiths, until George went on to be the tenant farmer at Hatch Farm [13] in the 1900s. By the time of the 1911 census, Albert Mills had moved into the Red House with his young family and had taken over the smithy.

Fig. 31. Harry and Edward Brown, blacksmiths.

Guardsman Cottages [18] d.

Next to the Red House stood a pair of semi-detached, timber-built cottages. These cottages and the next two properties [19 and 20] from 1852 to 1892 were owned by James Clarkson, and after his death, by his wife, Susanna [3].

At the rear of the cottages was a carpenter's workshop which, for at least 10 years (c.1861-71), was used by James Judd. Like many carpenters in a small rural community, Judd was asked to make coffins and act as the undertaker. The next occupant was Charles Boreham, also a carpenter and undertaker. He employed at least four men. Business did not go well for Boreham. In 1880 he was the plaintiff in a court case. He had been asked to make a coffin for one of the parishioners, but payment had not been forthcoming from the relatives.[73] He won that case, but six years later he was

Fig. 32. Guardsman Cottages.

adjudged bankrupt with debts of £199 and with assets of only £30. He admitted to failing to keep proper books of account and continuing to trade knowing that he was insolvent. After rearranging his affairs, he was lucky to be discharged in October of the same year. He then moved to Swindon where he could make a fresh start, but still as a carpenter.

Guardsman [19] d.

Fig. 33. Guardsman.

Next to these cottages was the Guardsman, a brick and tiled house with an attached shop (Fig. 33 is from the 1930s). Built c.1788, by 1829 it had become a wheelwright's. It then became a general store, and for a time, also the post office. By the 1880s it was also licensed to sell beer for consumption off the premises. George Powe became tenant in 1882 after taking over from Joseph Rorke [14].[75] Powe named it the Guardsman after his earlier career. He had joined the Grenadier Guards in 1858 and served his country for 21 years. He left the Guardsman in 1886 and became the licensee of the Swan Inn [67], across the common in Doddinghurst. He was still drawing his army pension in 1932, at the age of 95.[76]

Cottages [20] *d.*

Fig. 34. Cottage.

A little further along were two cottages. One originated from the late-eighteenth century and the other was built in the 1840s. It is not known which cottage is shown in Fig.34. There was also a large shed or barn next to the cottages. By 1834, the first cottage was in the ownership of George Sarling, a blacksmith, who may have worked in the nearby smithy [17] with his son, James. Later, both of these cottages were occupied by agricultural labourers and associated occupations. James Sarling remained living in one of these cottages, and on the 1871 census it is noted that he was 'blind with one eye'. This was probably the result of an occupational hazard: working in the smithy one day, a hot spark had landed on one of his eyes.

Caton's Cottages [21] *d.*

Behind these cottages and a little further back off the road, were three timber-built, plaster and lathe terraced cottages. They were known as Caton's Cottages and named after their owner and landlord. There were three rooms in each with a shared washhouse and gardens, and were occupied by agricultural workers.[77] One of them was Cornelius Burgess. Burgess was born in the parish in 1818 to William and Mary Burgess. He had two brothers, Rueben and George. In 1839 he married a local girl, Sarah Smith. The following year both of his parents died within a month of each other and Burgess took over responsibility of looking after his two brothers. The brothers later left home, and Cornelius and Sarah went on to have five children: Emma, Charlotte, Mary, George and William. In October 1860, tragedy struck the family. Within a month, Emma (18), Charlotte (16), William (4), and George (10) had died of diphtheria. Only Mary managed to survive. Their mother, no doubt heartbroken, died four years later. The records do not reveal what happened to Mary, but it is known that soon after his wife's death, Burgess sought help at the workhouse. It is not known whether he was unable to find work or was unable to work through illness. Whatever the reason, he remained in the workhouse until his death in 1877.

Well Cottage [22] *d.*

In the adjacent plot of land was a white, timber-boarded cottage known in 1911 as Well Cottage. Probably dating from the eighteenth century, it was occupied by various families including a shoemaker named James Ffitch who employed his two young sons in the business (1871); and James Sawkins who was a hay carter and a coal dealer (1901-1911). There was also an adjoining barn or shed for storage.

Fig. 35. Ongar Road in the early 1920s. The cottage immediately to the right of the war memorial is Well Cottage.

Fig. 36. Ongar Road, taken between 1906 and 1909.

On the right is the post office [16], Weal's Cottages [12], and Hatch Farm [13]. On the left can be seen part of Well Cottage [22]; one of the cottages [20]; the Guardsman [19]; the Red House [17]; and in the far distance, the church [55].

Part 3

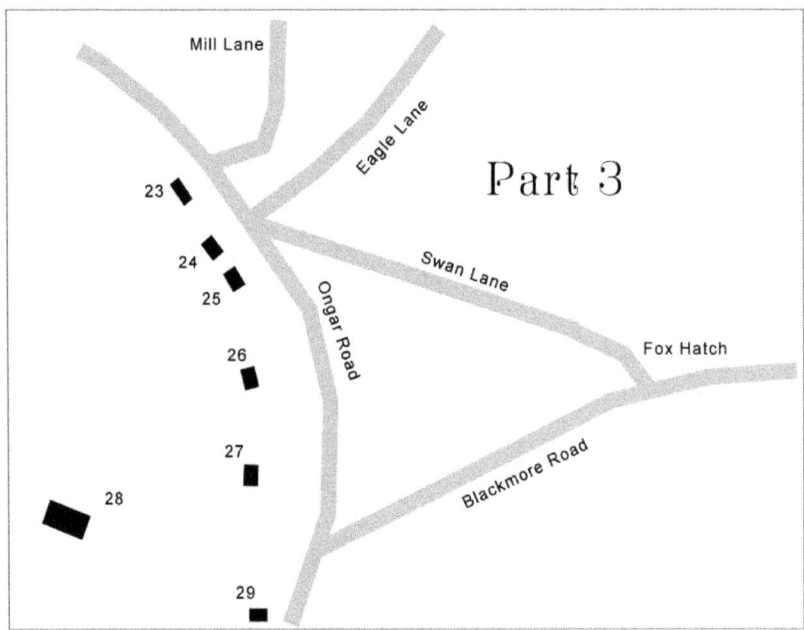

Fig. 37.

White House [23]

Continuing south down the Ongar Road for a 100 yards or so, on the right is the property known as the White House. The tithe map of 1838 shows there were two separate terraces of cottages on this piece of land, but by the time of the 1873 Ordnance Survey map, only one terrace is marked. The remaining terrace consisted of three cottages[78] and was occupied by various agricultural workers and artisans. At the turn of the century it was renovated, modernised, and converted into one dwelling with the new name of the White House. It was occupied in 1911 by Thomas Smith, a retired wheelwright; his wife, Eliza; and their daughter, Eleanor, who taught at the school.

Eagle Inn [24]

The next property along the Ongar Road is the Eagle Inn. It is difficult to date the building because of a gap in the manorial records, but records do show that in 1830 it was a cottage occupied by 'widow Brown', and that by 1838 it had been converted to an inn with a license to supply spirits, wines and beers.[79] The parish had been without a public house since c.1815 when 'The Compasses' was destroyed by fire (location not established).

Fig. 38. Eagle Inn in 1909 or 1910.

In 1886, the Eagle Inn was described as 'brick-built and tiled, contains beer and wine cellars, bar, taproom, kitchen, washhouse, and two bedrooms …attached to the front is a timber and slated parlour…the outbuildings comprise stable, cart shed, and skittle ground'.[80] The original outbuildings had been the target of an arson attack in 1848, during the time William Gandy was the licensee. The culprit was never found despite the offer of a £120 reward for information.[81]

The ownership of the Eagle changed many times, as did the licensees - some stayed for only a year or two - to list them all here would make for very tedious reading. One to mention, however, is in the photograph (Fig.38) (which has been retouched to remove earlier alterations). To the right of the door is George Palmer. He was a farmer from Ely and then later at Birdbrook. Standing at the door and wearing an apron is his youngest son, Albert, the licensee from 1909 to 1910. The females are believed to be George's daughters, Elizabeth and Bertha.

The Eagle was the centre of the social life for the commoners until the school and church room became an alternative. The inn is mentioned many times in newspaper articles: drunkenness, arguments, fights, petty crime, auctions and celebrations. One such celebration was at the end of the Crimean War in 1855. John Francis Wright of Kelvedon Hall [51] and the Countess of Waldegrave, who lived at Dudbrook Hall, arranged for the 'large

Fig. 39. Eagle Inn c.1910.

Photograph taken from Swan Lane, opposite the Eagle Inn.

building at the back of the Eagle' to be the venue for a celebratory dinner at which 86 parishioners attended. The band of the East India Company provided the music, while the guests enjoyed a fine meal. Afterwards, there were toasts to the royalty of Great Britain and France, and the singing of some patriotic songs.[82]

The Eagle was also the venue for coroner's inquests with the body being temporarily placed in one of the outbuildings ready for the coroner and jury to view. Newspaper reports of these inquests are often interesting because they provide a glimpse into the everyday life of the parishioners.

Between 1874 and 1890, there were at least eight coroner's inquests held in the Eagle inquiring into sudden deaths which occurred in the parish. The most notable was after a fire at Priors [62] which we will come to later. Two other inquests must have been very distressing as they involved young children. The Gould family had come from London to visit their relatives, the Quilter family. The Gould's daughter, Fanny, was playing on a swing with her one-year-old brother sat on her lap when the rope broke. They both fell forward onto the ground in a heap. The poor baby died instantly from a fractured skull.[83] The other inquest was into the sad case of Charles Hammond, a five-year-old suffering from sickness and diarrhoea for several days. His parents had administered castor oil but failed to seek medical help. During the inquest, the deputy coroner criticised the parents for failing to seek medical assistance and also commented on the fact that 'the child had not been baptised, showing a general indifference and neglect'. There were further observations on an open ditch close to their cottage which he described as offensive, and that their cottage, consisting of only one room, 'was altogether unfit for the habitation of a family'.[84] It is believed that this cottage was located at Old Crown End [43].

Cottage [25] *d.*

Stood next to the Eagle, in what is now its garden, was a cottage. Between 1841 and 1861, it was occupied by William Cooper and his family. Cooper was a master builder and employed at least three men. In the manorial records reference is made to this cottage burning down in the late 1870s, but, strangely, no newspaper reports of the fire can be found.

Woodlands [26]

Fig. 40. Woodlands.

Further along the Ongar Road is the house known as Woodlands. This house was built in the late-fifteenth century and is one of the oldest in the parish. Owned by the Kelvedon Hall estate, in 1920 it was described as 'containing two sitting rooms, kitchen, back kitchen, scullery, three bedrooms, [with an] earth closet, well, cart shed and stables.'[85] At the rear of the property were two fields, making the whole plot almost four acres. The photograph above (Fig. 40) is of the Porter family, it also shows that the house was weather-boarded; this was a recent addition, an earlier photograph shows the outside with exposed timber-frames and plaster walls.

Fig. 41. Members of the Porter family. They also appear in Fig.40.

Their identities are not confirmed, but they may be Jesse and Sarah Porter.

In the mid-nineteenth century, the house was occupied by the Smith family who farmed the few acres. Then sometime before 1861, William Porter and his wife, Sarah, moved in. Porter became a woodman on the Kelvedon Hall estate, as did his son and grandson. The Porters were to have nine children. When they grew up and married, some remained living in the house with their own children. For over 40 years this house was occupied by four generations of the extended Porter family.

As woodmen, the Porters were responsible for maintaining the woods on the estate: tree planting, coppicing, felling, and preparing the timber for sale. An auction was held in 1868 on behalf of the estate, it consisted of '40 ash trees, of good dimension and excellent quality; 5,000 faggots; 4,200 capital Ash and Alder Poles; 250 Hornbeam seconds; 150 bundles of Thatching Rods; 100 bundles of Pea Sticks.'[86] This list shows that despite the industrial revolution, wood still formed an important part of the agricultural economy, and that several workers would have been involved in the preparation of these woodland products.

The Chase [27]

Next to Woodlands is a large house now known as The Chase. It had acquired this name by 1911 because of its association with fox hunting. During the nineteenth century it was known as Keatings, after its owner and occupier, John Keating and his wife, Elizabeth, who acquired the house in the 1820s. He was a merchant dealing in corn, tea and tobacco.[87] After his early death in 1834 at the age of 32,[88] Elizabeth remained a widow for the rest of her life. She died in 1884 at the age of 81.[89] One of her children, John, a surveyor, predeceased her in 1881; and Anna, her daughter, inherited the house and a number of properties in the parish. Anna died in 1893.

The property was then advertised for sale with the following description: 'small residential property or Hunting Box, substantial brick-built and slated dwelling house with large and productive kitchen and pleasure gardens, two orchards, stabling for 3 horses, chaise-house and outbuildings, within easy reach of three packs of hounds.'[90] [91] This emphasis on hunting was aimed at a gentleman living and working in London and who wished to take part in country pursuits within easy reach of London. Kelvedon Common had been the meeting place for fox hunting throughout the century. Meeting at the windmill twice a week at 11 am, the hunt set off in search of its prey, ranging widely over the surrounding countryside - sometimes followed by schoolboys who had bunked-off school.[92]

In 1913, the house was occupied by Lieut. Colonel Sidney Goss Mullock of the Essex Regiment, and his wife, Margaret. They had been married for four years and had two children. Mullock no doubt chose The Chase for its convenient distance from Warley Barracks where his regiment was garrisoned. Mullock was killed in France in 1917. Margaret remarried the following year.

Brizes [28]

Leaving The Chase and continuing down the Ongar Road, on the right is Brizes. This is the first of three grand mansions visited on the tour. Brizes was built in the 1720s by the Glassock family. The estate, however, dates back to at least the fifteenth century and is named after its medieval owner, Thomas Bryce. After the Glassock family, the estate passed to Charles Dolby, and then to his brother, William. His children in turn inherited the estate until their deaths: Charles in 1826, age 60; Jane in 1855, age 82; and Louisa in 1868, age 90. During their time at Brizes, the Dolby family were generous to the parishioners. Jane and Louisa gave 'weekly during the winter months meat, coals, and bread, to the neighbouring poor';[93] and Louisa left in her will £100 for 'the poor of the parish'. This eventually became part of the Poor's Charity [4].

The Dolby sisters were elderly spinsters when the modern Victorian world suddenly arrived unannounced at Brizes. In the mid-Victorian period, ballooning was very much in its infancy and the sight of a balloon must have been an exciting moment for a country person who had never seen one before. In 1852, a balloon with its passengers was launched from Cremorne Gardens, a popular leisure garden in Chelsea, and it made its way across London and Essex until the pilot executed an emergency landing in the grounds of Brizes. The reaction of the Dolby's is not recorded, but it caused 'quite a sensation in the locality'.[94] With assistance of the 'wondering locals' the balloon was secured and loaded on a cart, and the pilot and passengers made their way back to London by train from Brentwood.[95]

Fig. 42. Brizes during the time of the Dolbys.

Fig. 43. Brizes, after installation of the greenhouses.

When the Dolby sisters died there were no children to inherit the estate, so by the terms of William Dolby's will, the estate passed down his wife's family line to a John Royds who already possessed his own estate, albeit much smaller, in Fleet, Hampshire. The Misses Dolby had also owned several cottages in Kelvedon Hatch and Doddinghurst, and when John Royds arrived he set about purchasing further properties and land in the area, and enfranchising the copyhold land he already owned. He also added to the mansion house the greenhouses seen in Fig.43, many of which were to be later smashed in the great hailstorm of 1897 [13].

Royds became a JP and sat as a magistrate in Brentwood, and in common with other owners of large mansion houses, he employed several servants. This example is from the 1871 census. Attending to the needs of John Royds and his wife, Eliza, was a housekeeper, two housemaids, a laundry-maid, kitchen-maid, dairy-maid, lady's maid, butler, footman, head groom and an under-groom. Missing from the list you will notice is the cook. Perhaps she was away on the night of the census.

After John Royds' death in 1884 at the age of 81, the estate passed to his brother, the Revd Charles Leopold Royds. At the age of 68, Charles with his wife, Catherine, left his vicarage in Aldenham and moved into the grander surroundings of Brizes. The Revd Royds soon became involved in parish affairs. As well as providing a temporary home for the parish room, he donated land on which the new parish church could be built. In 1887, he hosted the Queen Victoria's jubilee celebrations in the grounds of Brizes at which 200 adults and 90 children attended. They sat down to a dinner consisting of 'cold joints, hot potatoes, and plum puddings.' The queen was then toasted and the national anthem sung. There then followed various sports, and the day was rounded off with a display of fireworks.[96]

Charles Royds died in 1896, and his son, Charles Duncan Royds, succeeded to the estate. He also took part in parish affairs. Apart from being a JP, he was a member of the parish council, active in church affairs, and chairman of the board of managers of the school (from which he later resigned following a spat over building alterations to the school, describing the county council's management of the school as a 'pantomime').[97] We shall read more of Charles Royds and a dispute with a neighbour, a little later.

Brizes Lodge [29]

Surprisingly, Brizes did not have a lodge at the entrance gates until 1909.[98] In 1911 the lodge was occupied by Stanley Roberts and his family. Roberts was the chauffeur to Charles Royds.

Part 4

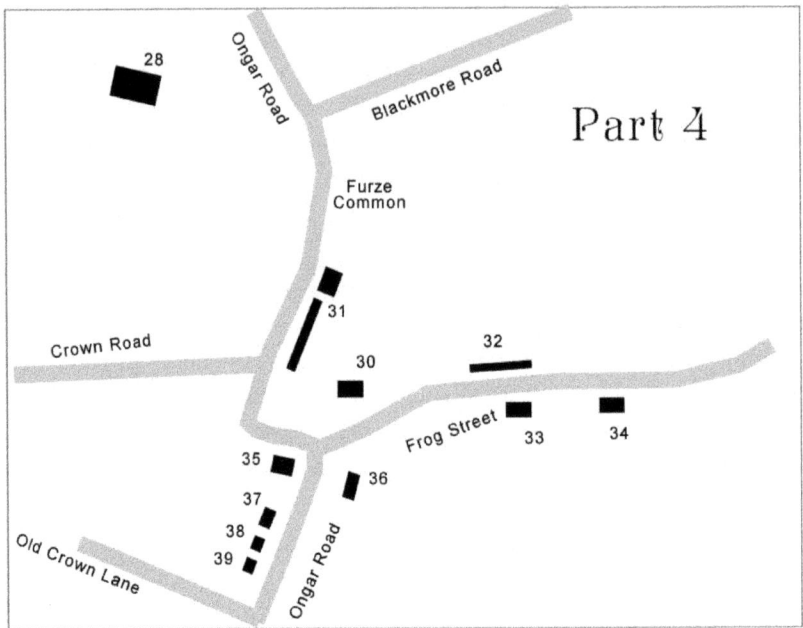

Fig. 44.

Orchard Dene [30]

The tour now jumps forward on its route, past Pheasant Lodge, Park View, the Thorns and the Briars [31]. This is to easier understand the narrative for the development of these properties. Further down the Ongar Road, on the left is a footpath. Turning onto the footpath, on the right is Farrington House [35], and on the left, Orchard Dene.

The land on which Orchard Dene stood was created earlier from an enclosure of the common land in the seventeenth or eighteenth centuries. By 1838, it was owned by a John Smith and leased to a tenant farmer, William Dunnings, who farmed the 10 acres. Unfortunately, no description of the original house survives, nor do we know when the house gained its name. After Dunnings, it was farmed by Henry Newcombe, a former blacksmith from East Horndon. His two sons were mentioned previously at Hatch Farm [13]. He lived here with his wife, Eliza, who died in the 1850s, and then with his daughter, Marian, until his death in 1878.

There is now a gap in the records until 1887. It is thought that during this period a new house was built on the site because in 1875 a newspaper article refers to the parish surveyor wishing to gain access to the land to survey it as a possible source of gravel for the parish roads. At the time, Newcombe refused admission saying, 'the landlord was intending to build a new house and any gravel pit may interfere with its construction'.[99] It is not known what happened regarding the surveyor, but it does seem that a new house was built – and an unusual one at that. In 1899, the house was described as being large, and built on the 'American bungalow principal and entirely composed of wood and iron, with a corrugated tin roof'[100] – an unusual design in late-Victorian England.

At this time the house was occupied by Lewis Hopcraft and his family. They had moved to the parish around 1887. Hopcraft became involved in community affairs and in 1894 he was the first chairman of the newly created parish council. Hopcraft was also an inventor and businessman. For some years he had been filing patents for improved furnaces and fire-grates, and even for improvements to bicycle brakes. A few years earlier, his daughter had married one of the sons of Giuseppe Garibaldi, the Italian general and politician who fought for a unified Italy. His son-in-law was also a soldier and had fought with Garibaldi. A great deal of interest was created in the parish when the couple came to visit their family.

On 23 February 1899, Hopcraft and his family were moving out of Orchard Dene to go to a new house in London. It turned out to be a disastrous moving day. Mrs Hopcraft and her children left to catch a train to London, while two vans arrived to collect the contents of the house. Suddenly a fire was discovered in the upper part of the house. Unable to extinguish the fire, the removers rushed to take the furniture outside. The fire brigade in Brentwood was telegraphed for, and after some difficulty in harnessing the horses, the fire engine arrived. While attempting to extinguish the fire a fireman was injured, and a change in wind direction threatened to turn the flames on the fire engine itself. The fire brigade's efforts, however, were in vain, the house was completely destroyed.[101]

It is not possible to describe the reactions of the new owner to this disaster, but we can say that a new bungalow was built on the spot. By 1901, the new owner, William Robert Godlonton Roebuck, a retired cabinet manufacturer, with his wife, Clarissa, and their 5 children, were in occupancy. From working class roots, William started a career in cabinet making and eventually owned his own factory, and employed at least two of his sons and a daughter in his sales team. He had recently moved from Plashet Hall in Newham, a grand Georgian house, so clearly he had achieved a great deal. On his death, his personal estate was worth over £34000.

Roebuck and Royds of Brizes did not get on as neighbours and the story of their dispute leads us on to the next houses on the tour.

Pheasant Lodge, Park View, The Thorns, The IOUs (later The Briars) [31], and The Avenue [32]

One day in January 1902, Roebuck was out shooting in an area of the old common owned by Royds which was known locally as Furze Common or Fuzzy Piece, now an area of woodland opposite Brizes. Perhaps thinking he was still on his own land, Roebuck shot a pheasant. It is not clear what happened next, but a short time after he was summonsed to appear before the magistrates at Ongar for killing a pheasant without a licence. He was fined £1 with costs of 7s 6d. His defence was that he had acted in ignorance.[102]

Roebuck clearly blamed Royds for the embarrassment of being taken before the court. He now sought a way to get his revenge. Roebuck built a pair of semi-detached houses which he named Pheasant Lodge and Park View. (Fig. 45) These houses could be clearly seen from Brizes and spoilt the view. Royds, it is said, responded by planting trees in his park to hide his view of the houses. Not to be thwarted, Roebuck built three rows of single-story terraced houses: two in the Ongar Road, and one on the other side of his land in Frog Street. The two terraces facing Brizes he named The Thorns and The IOUs (the latter was later renamed as The Briars). (Fig. 46) The names speak for themselves. Meanwhile, the terrace in Frog Street was given the more polite name of The Avenue. Royds' reaction or response to these is not known.

Apart from being motivated by revenge, Roebuck clearly saw that there was a chance to make money from this building development. Many cottages in the area were in a dilapidated condition and the offer of new housing at low rents would attract tenants. By 1907, he had built The Thorns and The Avenue properties, ten houses in each. Each house had four rooms which ranged in size from 12'x10' to 8'x6', with one wash-house shared between the occupants of five houses. Fresh water could be collected from a well dug in front of the properties, while a large rain-water tank at the rear of the properties provided water for other uses.[103] Rent for The Thorns was 3s 6d a week, while The Avenue, which had better gardens and situation, was 4s 6d a week.[104] By the time of the 1911 census, eighteen of these houses were occupied, many of them by parishioners who had moved from other cottages in the parish. For some of the tenants these cottages must have been a great improvement on their former homes, and yet not everyone was satisfied. In 1909, a complaint was made to the parish council and the District Sanitary Committee about the unsanitary conditions in the cottages. Following an inspection by the Sanitary Committee, it was found there was nothing wrong with the sanitary arrangements and that the 'complaint arose owing to the dirty habits of the tenants over which the District Council has no jurisdiction.'[105]

Fig.45. Pheasant Lodge and Park View.

A shop was built to the side of Pheasant Lodge which later became a tea room for passing cyclists and motorists.

Fig. 46. Ongar Road facing north showing the IOUs, and further on, The Thorns.

North View (later North Field) [33] *d.*

Opposite The Avenue in Frog Street was North View. Built in the early 1890s, all that is known about this house was that it was also a general store and bakery. Located on the parish border with Doddinghurst, it served the cottages and farms in the immediate vicinity. In 1890, it was occupied by William Willing, and his wife, Rachel. They were assisted by their lodger, Sydney Snow, a journeyman baker.

Cottages [34] *d.*

Next to North View stood a pair of semi-detached cottages. Dating from the early-nineteenth century and built on recently enclosed common land by Jeremiah Lagden, a farmer, they were occupied by agricultural workers. One of these was occupied by Walter Jordan, a hay binder and carter. Looking through the newspaper archives it seems that a prerequisite of the job of a hay carter was to sleep on the job – no doubt because of their long working days. There are numerous prosecutions of hay carters making their way through Kelvedon Hatch while fast asleep on their horse and cart, their horse treading a well-known path to Brentwood or Romford. Jordan fell asleep while crossing Romford Common and was later fined 2s 6d – an expensive sleep![106] Despite this minor set-back, Jordan went on to become a hay dealer and the licensee of the Shepherd [71].

Farrington House [35]

Returning now to Farrington House which was briefly mentioned earlier. Before the road was straightened in the twentieth century, the Ongar Road took an S-bend around Farrington House. This bend became known as Knightbridge Corner and was named after the owner of Farrington House. The house was built in 1855[107,] on a piece of the former common land which had been enclosed in the late-eighteenth century. It became the home and workplace of the Knightbridge family who were butchers. Henry Knightbridge was born in Stock, where his father was a butcher. Henry then moved to Kelvedon Hatch with his wife, Elizabeth. They were to have two daughters and eight sons. All his sons became butchers. As they grew up and married, six of them moved away to establish their own butchery businesses in Brentwood, Romford, Havering, Woodford, and Walthamstow. When Henry came to retirement, the Kelvedon Hatch butchery business was taken over by youngest son, William. They both served the community by variously becoming members of the parish vestry, later the parish council; founder member of the school board; and as churchwardens.

Fig. 47. The Knightbridge brothers ready to slaughter the ox.

The butchery skills of the Knightbridge family were called upon during the Queen Victoria's golden jubilee celebrations in Brentwood. A whole ox was roasted in the paddock of the Yorkshire Grey PH. It was slaughtered by master butcher Edwin Knightbridge and his brothers.

Virginia House [36]

Opposite Farrington House, on the other side of the former Ongar Road, is the house known as Virginia House. Known by this name by 1911, it consisted of eight rooms and had a small farm attached with a cowhouse, stabling, piggeries, and 9 acres of land.[108] The house dates from the early-eighteenth century and was built upon an early enclosure of the former common land. The acreage was too small to generate sufficient income from farming, so the occupants had other forms of income.

In the 1840s and 1850s, the farm was owned by the Moss family who also owned the windmill at Bentley in South Weald. Their tenant was Charles Grove and his wife, Mary Ann. Grove was also the miller at Bentley where he was assisted by his eldest son, William.

In the 1870s and 1880s, the tenant farmer was Henry Pain and his family. Pain was also a cow dealer and was part of an extended Pain family who lived in South Weald and Navestock. Pain owned a donkey named Toker. He bet a friend that his donkey with a rider could cover the ten miles from Writtle to Kelvedon Hatch in under an hour. The bet was taken up and the donkey, with Pain as the jockey, made the journey with only eight minutes to spare.[109]

Fig. 48. Ongar Road facing north c.1910.

Farrington House [35] left, and Virginia House [36] right. The modern road now goes to the left of Farrington House and there is a Chinese restaurant on the right.

Pain was also a keen horse racing man and would have enjoyed the Navestock Races. In the late-eighteenth century there had been horse racing at Navestock Side (to the east of the present cricket pitch and marked on a map of 1785). It then seems to have dropped out of use.[110] Horse racing was resumed in 1866 and lasted until 1878. The annual meet started off with three races, but by 1874 it had expanded to six races, and had considerable support from the horse-owning aristocracy. The race stewards and officials were members of the local gentry and these included John Royds of Brizes [28] and Edward Carrington Wright of Kelvedon Hall [51], while Pain's father acted as course supervisor (he was also licensee of the Green Man pub situated near the course and the cricket field).

But these annual races were to have a negative impact on the residents of Kelvedon Hatch and Navestock. The races attracted the criminal element of society, and after one meeting, the Essex Times noted that 'never before has Navestock been visited by such a gang of sharpers, welchers, and pickpockets, as swarmed the course on this occasion.'[111] During one meeting, Henry Newcombe's house [30] was broken into while he was at the races. He lost £20 in the burglary.[112] There were several other incidents of crime in other years and this may have been a contributory factor in the decision to cancel the annual races.

Kumra Lodge [37]

Fig. 49. Kumra Lodge taken around 1910.

Continuing south down the Ongar Road, on the right is the large house known as Kumra Lodge. Before 1882 it was known as Amy Cottage and then as Warren House. Late Georgian in style, it is difficult to date exactly because of a gap in the manorial records. The plot of land was enlarged following further enclosure of the common in 1836. Throughout the period it was occupied by the well-off middle class. The first known owner was Solomon Mentor and his wife, Sarah. He died in 1841, leaving her living here for a further 21 years. During this time she was employed as a schoolmistress, although it is not known where.

The next occupants were David Wilkin, a yeast merchant, who died in 1865, leaving his widow, Ann, living in the house until 1875. Moving in after them was William Mills Edmonds with his wife, Eliza, and six of their children. Edmonds was a wholesale button and trimming manufacturer. Perhaps Edmonds was attracted to the parish by the transport links to London. By this time there was a regular omnibus service between Brentwood Station and Ongar Station. Edmonds lived in the house until 1883.

Arthur Stronge Gilbert, a retired army major, then took up occupancy with his wife, Melvina. The arrival of this couple must have caused a stir in local society because Melvina was an Indian Princess. Her full title before her marriage was the Princess Melvina Rundhir Singh Ahluwalia, daughter of his Highness the late Rajah Rundhir Singh, of Kapurthala, Punjab, and his Anglo-Indian wife.[113] Gilbert met her while serving in India. After a wedding ceremony in Paris, and then for some reason, a further ceremony in Epsom, they moved into the house which they then renamed Kumra Lodge. Later that year they had a son, Arthur Stuart Ahluwalia Stronge Gilbert. When an adult, Arthur joined the Indian Civil Service and became a close friend of the Irish writer, James Joyce, and translated many of his works into French. The Gilbert's moved to Cheltenham in 1893. There then followed a quick turnover of several other occupants.

Cottage [38]

Next to Kumra Lodge was a pair of semi-detached cottages, and constructed at about the same time as Kumra Lodge. It is not clear whether the present house, Kinglsey Cottage, is the original building or a replacement. These cottages were occupied by various agricultural workers and artisans, and in 1901, by the village policeman, Alfred Medcalf.

This is now a suitable time to look at policing in Kelvedon Hatch during this period. Under the parish vestry system, two or three of its members were appointed constable. These were often tradesmen such as a blacksmith, wheelwright, or carpenter. These men were strong individuals, both physically and in their personality. They dealt with any crime or disturbance in the parish and had the power to bring any wrong-doer before a magistrate. This system, however, could not cope with the changes underway in Victorian society caused by industrialisation and improved transportation, and so they made way for the professional police force.

The Essex Constabulary was formed in February 1840 following the passing of the Rural Police Act. As the name suggests, their role was mainly rural policing. The Act did not cover the county borough towns of Maldon and Colchester which had their own borough constables. With an establishment of a little over 200 men, the county was split into divisions, then detachments, then guards or beats. The officers not only involved themselves in crime prevention and public order, but they also supervised weights and measures; common lodging-houses; vagrants; and under the Poor Law, were assistant relieving officers. As the century advanced, the number of officers was increased.

Kelvedon Hatch came under Brentwood division and the police officer responsible for Kelvedon Hatch and Doddinghurst lived in the community in various houses as there was no local police station. Even when officially off-duty, they could be called upon by a parishioner knocking on their door and informing them of something untoward in the parish. At first this new rural police force was generally unwelcome in Kelvedon Hatch. The parish vestry minutes from 1842 record that its members voted 'to get rid of the system' of rural police as 'the services rendered by the Rural Police are so disproportionate to the expense they bring upon the rate payers.'[114] But the rate payers were to find that the police force was here to stay.

A search through the newspaper archives reveals a number of Kelvedon Hatch cases in which the police officers were involved. Apart from one distressing case of murder at Langford Bridge Cottages [57], most revolve around cases of petty theft, poaching, and dealing with drunks. What is revealed in these cases is that the officer was very much on their own if there was a problem. In a case of needing urgent assistance, a message would have to have sent by foot or by horse rider to the Brentwood or Ongar Police Stations. Help could take up to two or three hours to arrive. For example, Constable Medcalf arrested three poachers and held them at the Swan Inn [67] until transport could be arranged. While he was waiting, he was jostled and abused by some local labourers, but fortunately for him, they did not attempt to rescue their friends. Another problem was mobility. Getting from one end of the parish to the other on foot on winter roads could take up to an hour. The fight against crime was helped by the arrival of the telegraph and the bicycle. In 1894, using his bicycle, Constable Medcalf pursued, overtook and arrested two soldiers who were on foot after they had committed a robbery. Another thing the articles show is how strangers, especially vagrants and soldiers, were immediately noticed by the local police officer and parishioners, and treated with great suspicion until they left the parish.

From the records of the Essex Constabulary[115] and the census returns, some of the officers who were stationed at Kelvedon Hatch can be identified:

1851 - Collar number 57. William Fuller, a former shoemaker, joined the force in 1842. Soon after being transferred from Kelvedon Hatch he was discharged having been found on licensed premises while on duty.

1861 - Collar number 30. William Warne, a former gamekeeper, joined the force in 1852 and retired after 25 years' service.

1861 - 1872 Collar number 189. Joseph Davey, a former labourer, joined the force in 1857 and served at Kelvedon Hatch for eleven years until his sudden death in 1872.

1881 - 1882 Collar number 137. Joseph Archer, a former blacksmith, joined the force in 1871, but was dismissed in 1882 for drunkenness.

1887 - 1902 Collar number 40. Alfred Medcalf joined the force in 1885. In 1887 was transferred to Kelvedon Hatch. It appears that he was well thought of during his time in the parish for upon his transfer he was presented with a gold watch by the grateful parishioners.[116]

1904 - 1905 Collar number 177. Albert Hayward, transferred after being disciplined for neglect of duty.

1911 - 1919 Collar number 312. Edward Barrett, a former soldier, was transferred from Wethersfield after he was found to be drunk while off-duty, but otherwise he had an unblemished record during his time at Kelvedon Hatch.

Rose Cottage [39]

Fig. 50. Rose Cottage and Kingsley Cottage.

Next to Kingsley Cottage was Rose Cottage (both are seen in this photograph from the early 1930s). Built c.1840, on the recently enclosed common land, in 1896 it was described as 'a good residence with large garden and orchard, stabling for three horses, outhouses, two cowsheds, with five of acres of land'.[117] It became a middle-class home with occupants such as Joseph Cliff, a retired farmer (1841); Colonel Conway (1851); Frederick Moss, owner of the mill at Bentley (1861); Alfred Clyatt, a journalist who for 60 years reported on proceedings at the Old Bailey and attended every hanging which took place under that court's jurisdiction (1871);[118] and Henry Smith, farmer and dealer (1881).

In 1896, the property was purchased by William Henry Brown (in the photograph), who, with his wife, Clare, converted some of the farm buildings and operated a laundry business. It operated at least until his death in 1936. The house was badly damaged by a bomb in World War Two and had to be rebuilt.

Part 5

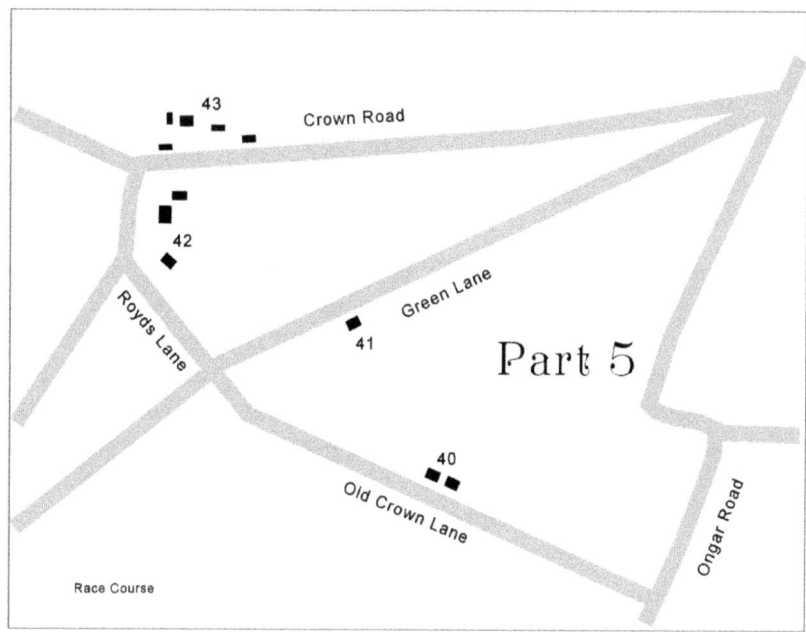

Fig. 51.

Cottages [40] part *d*.

The route now turns right off the Ongar Road and down Old Crown Lane. Before the enclosures, this was a trackway across the common and followed the Kelvedon Hatch – South Weald boundary. Halfway down the lane, on the right-hand side, was a cottage and a pair of semi-detached cottages, both let out at cheap rents to agricultural labours. Both were built c.1860. The single cottage has since been demolished, while it is believed the other pair have been greatly altered and extended.

One of these cottages was occupied for over 40 years by Jeremiah Beadle and his wife, Sarah. In another cottage lived the Enever family. For one of their sons, George Enever (age 42), there is a vivid description of him in a court report. Brought before the Ongar magistrates for theft of three live tame rabbits, the court reporter described him as having 'a wooden leg, no coat, hair lengthy [and] presented a singular appearance.' Of his life-style, a police officer observed that: 'he sleeps in pig styes, picks up manure and anything he can find, and spends most of his time in the public house'. Another witness described him as an 'artful, cunning man'.[119]

Cottage [41]

Continuing down Old Crown Lane, we come to a crossroads. To the left, the lane leads to Navestock Side, and to the right, the lane turns into a footpath which comes out by Crown Corner. This lane is known as Green Lane. Before the common was enclosed, this was the road to Romford. Here on the right, built between 1884 and 1897 on land owned by the Brizes estate, was a timber-built cottage with a stable and cart shed.[120] The house has since been rebuilt and is now known as Woodberry.

Old Crown / Crownfields / Cottages [42] *part d.*

Returning now to the crossroads, the tour continues down Royds Lane until the junction with Navestock Side. This is the border with Navestock parish. This area of the parish was known as Old Crown End or Old Crown Corner. On the right lies Crownfields, a former farm house originally called Old Crown. Parts of the property date from the seventeenth century, and this may have been the same building in which there was an alehouse called The Crown during the early half of the eighteenth century. For a short time it also went by the name of Lovelands, after James Love who owned it in the early 1830s. In 1835, after his death, it was described as a 'brick-built dwelling house, sash-windows, entrance-hall, two parlours, three chambers, two attics, kitchen, dairy, and three cellars, [with a] large detached brewhouse, farm yard, barn, two stables, cowhouse, and orchard with 70 trees.'[121] The farm consisted of two acres of arable and six acres of meadow land. This was increased to 10 acres after the enclosure of the common land.

From 1870 to 1884, the property was part of the Brizes estate [28] and let yearly for £12 to Archer Samuel, a builder and bricklayer, who lived there with his wife, Amy. They also had a long-term lodger by the name of Ann Noakes, who in 1871, described herself as a school mistress with 18 pupils. It is not known where she taught them, but it may have been in this house.

Within the grounds were two cottages: one of four rooms, the other with two bedrooms, sitting room, two pantries, kitchen and wash-house.[122] These were occupied by agricultural workers who worked on the farm. One family, the Firbanks, worked on the farm from at least 1841 to 1871. John Firbank was a long-lived resident of the parish: Kelvedon Hatch born and bred, he died aged 80. One of these cottages was later demolished. It was replaced by new accommodation called Half a Crown and was occupied by servants and gardeners for the main house.

When the property was sold in 1884, it was purchased by John Thomas Newman. Newman was an architect and a fellow member of the Royal Institute of Architects (RIBA) He extended and modernised the property turning it into a desirable middle-class home with parts of the former farm

Fig. 52. Crownfields.

land turned into gardens. He also changed its name to Crownfields. In 1923 the house was described as a 'hall, three reception rooms, domestic offices, cellar, [and] seven bed and dressing rooms.'[123] Newman had commenced his independent architectural practice in 1865 and became architect to the West Ham and Leyton School Boards, and the London Hospital Estates. In the parish, meanwhile, his architectural services were called upon in the refurbishment of the old St Nicholas's Church in 1887; and when a new church was proposed, he drew up the design, provided detailed plans, liaised with the builders and supervised its construction – all donated free. He died in 1896, shortly after the new church was opened.

The above photograph (Fig. 52) was taken c.1910. The girl in the picture may be Ivy Earthy, daughter of the occupier of the house at that time: Walter Earthy, a bank manager or senior bank clerk.

Old Crown Cottage and Cottages [43] *part d.*

Opposite Crownfields was a number of cottages – believed to be five. Four of them were built before 1800. These buildings were closely grouped together so it has been difficult to identify each individual cottage and its occupants until near the end of the nineteenth century. In the 1830s, these cottages were owned by the Kelvedon Hall estate and let out to agricultural workers. As the century progressed, most of the properties were sold and became freehold, and one new small brick-built cottage was added (now Crownside Cottage).

Some of these cottages were in a terrible condition. In 1879, Henry Adams, a labourer, fell down the stairs in one of the cottages. At the inquest the coroner made some 'severe remarks upon the state of the house, which was considered unfit for a pig to live in'.[124] At another coroner's inquest held at the Eagle Inn [24], remarks were made about the poor condition of another of the cottages.

After these inquests, one of the cottages underwent extensive renovation and rebuilding, while another of the cottages was converted to an outbuilding for storage. The outcome by 1895 was that one cottage could now be better described as a house and suited for middle-class occupants: 'three reception rooms, kitchen, scullery, three bedrooms, servants attic, two stall stables, coach house, harness room, standing in an acre of well-furnished garden with tennis lawn.'[125] This house is now known as Crownside, but in the early twentieth century it was known for a short time as the Firs.

Fig. 53. Rebecca Thomas.

One person living in this group of cottages was Rebecca Thomas. Born in Kelvedon Hatch, she lived in the parish all her life, most of it in one of these cottages. She died in 1921, at the age of 100. Despite improved transport links and opportunities in the expanding towns and cities, there were still some parishioners who, like Thomas, spent all their lives in the parish. During this period, outside of Essex there was held the general perception that Essex was damp and unhealthy. In 1880, the rector took the trouble of writing to a newspaper pointing out that this was clearly wrong for he had recently buried five people with the average age of 82: 'widow Beadle, 79; James Benton, 80; George Bodgby, 90; widow Maddox, 80; and William Porter, 83.'[126] He did not, however, point out that the childhood death rates were still very high.

Also living in one of these cottages in the 1860s was the Rainbird family. Two of their sons, Thomas (14) and Zachariah (16), were brought before the magistrates' court for threatening the parish surveyor. Before going into the case any further, it would be useful to describe how the parish roads were maintained. At this time, the parish vestry was responsible for the maintenance of all the roads within its boundaries. Two of its members were appointed surveyors. Their responsibilities were: to ensure the roads were maintained to a satisfactory standard; to employ labourers to make repairs; source suitable road building material; ensure there were adequate road signs; and to clear the roads of snow if they were blocked. In 1881, a severe snow storm engulfed the parish. The surveyor at the time, James French of Langford Bridge Farm [56], organised a gang of labourers to clear the roads.[127] In the school log book the head teacher recorded: 'On Tuesday last such a snow storm and hurricane of wind occurred as no one could remember the like of. The following morning roads were so blocked that traffik [sic] was entirely suspended. Fifty men were set to make a cartway through the parish before it could be resumed. Where the snow had drifted, it was, in places, eleven and twelve feet in depth, into which many wayfarers had fallen and some, who had not the fortune to be extricated, were found dead.'[128]

The roads were used by hundreds of horses during the year, and, as one can imagine, a considerable amount of horse manure was deposited on them. Some of it dried on the road and the rest was pushed to the verges. It was discovered that scraping the top surface of the road and collecting the debris on the side of the road (known as drift) produced a rich organic material which farmers could spread on their fields as a fertiliser. This was recognised to be a potential source of income for parishes, so by virtue of the Highways Act of 1835, the parish vestry owned the road scrapings and drift. Every year the parish roads were split into sections and local farmers submitted tenders for the annual right to collect the scrapings and drift. This was a useful source of income for the parish to spend on the upkeep of the roads.

Returning now to the two Rainbird brothers, they were found by Henry Newcombe, the parish surveyor, gathering road scrapings – no doubt to add to their family's vegetable plots. Upon being told they were doing wrong, they 'threatened to split his head open with their shovel if he dared touch them'. They were fined 5s each.[129]

Following highways legislation in 1867 and 1878, Kelvedon Hatch was amalgamated with a number of surrounding parishes for the purpose of road maintenance. This system was abolished in 1894 by the creation of the Ongar Rural District Council (RDC) which then took on responsibility for the maintenance of roads. At the lower level of local administration, the parish vestry was abolished and parish councils created. In the following years the parish council minutes are peppered with complaints about the bad state of the roads in the parish and their poor maintenance by the RDC.

Fig. 54. The windmill.
This unknown lady would step carefully as the roads were always covered in horse manure.

Part 6

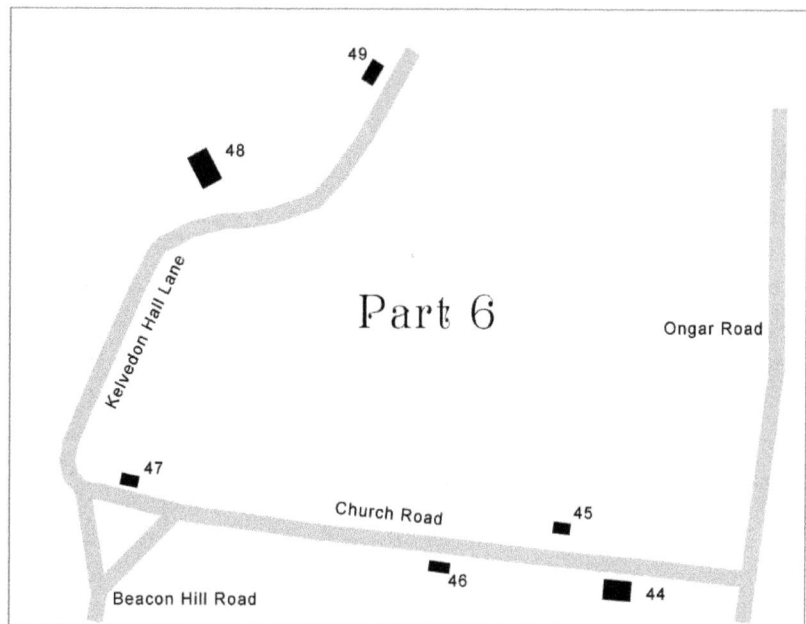

Fig. 55.

Dodds Farm [44]

The tour now returns to Church Road (formerly known as Dodds Road), and recommences at Dodds Farm. This farm house dates from the fifteenth century. There have been many improvements and alterations to the house since then. In 1884, the farm consisted of 50 acres across both Kelvedon Hatch and Navestock. The house, meanwhile, contained two sitting rooms, a large kitchen with an oven, pantries, cellars, and six bedrooms.[130]

Known also at this time as Willows Farm, from c.1837 to 1851, the farm was owned by John Sympson Jessopp, barrister-at-law, Deputy-Lieutenant of Essex and JP. Jessopp held a considerable property portfolio across Essex and Hertfordshire. Upon his death, the farm was purchased for £1580 and became part of the Brizes estate for the remainder of the nineteenth century. Occupied by various tenant farmers and agricultural workers, at one time it was split into two properties, and as we have seen, these briefly became the venue for the village club [14], and the home of the postmaster Frederick Brenes [16].

Cottage [45] *d.*

A little further down Church Road, on the opposite side of the road to Dodds Farm, stood a pair of semi-detached cottages. Owned by the Kelvedon Hall estate, they had been demolished by 1920, probably because they were unfit for habitation. During this period they were occupied by agricultural workers and their families. Otherwise, nothing else is known about them.

Willow Row [46]

Continuing down Church Road, on the left is a cottage now known as Willow Cottage. Originally three terraced cottages, each cottage consisted of four rooms with the occupants sharing a common wash-house and bakehouse.[131] These cottages were occupied by various agricultural workers and their families. One of them was the Jarvis family. They are mentioned several times in the archives, and these records give us a brief glimpse into their lives.

William Jarvis and his wife, Sarah, were both born in Stapleford Abbotts, and they married in Havering in 1832. By 1841 they had moved to Kelvedon Hatch, and in 1861 were living in Willow Row. William worked as an agricultural labourer all his life, while Sarah brought up their eight children, as well as working in the fields herself. In 1854, William had to look after the children himself as Sarah had stolen a loaf of bread and was sentenced to six weeks' hard labour.[132] When their children reached adulthood, some married and remained living in the parish, while the unmarried adults remained in the family home.

Apart from Sarah's problems with the law, they would have seen a police officer at their door on many occasions in connection with their children, sometimes for distressing reasons. One son, James, was arrested on at least three occasions for poaching; while their other son, John, had a drink problem. On three occasions there are court reports about his drunkenness. But these were minor troubles compared with what was to come. In 1880, their second eldest son, Henry, was working in the fields when he stopped for a drink of water. He then became giddy, collapsed and foamed at the mouth. He was taken to the doctor who diagnosed he was suffering from 'nervous exhaustion' and prescribed weak brandy and water, and rest. Within hours, Henry was dead. The doctor considered that death arose 'from congestion of the brain, caused by shock to the system from drinking cold water when extremely hot'[133] (this reveals the state of the medical knowledge at the time.) Their youngest son, Arthur, died in 1886 following an accident. While working with a traction engine, he fell and the wheels passed over his leg completely crushing it. He was taken to the infirmary at Chelmsford where his leg was amputated, but he died soon after.[134]

One of their two daughters who lived at home was Abigail. She was described as an 'indifferent character' when she appeared before magistrates' court for a second offence of violence. It is clear from the report of the court proceedings that she was a woman who held a grudge against a fellow female farm worker whom she 'rendered insensible' by a barrage of blows.[135] Abigail never married, but she did have five children, one of whom died at the age of two months. When the first four were baptised, the father's name was not given. At the baptism of the last child, after Abigail's death, the surname of Challis was given to the child. All four surviving children would have the stigma of being a bastard, and the eldest, Alice, suffered even more.

A close neighbour of the Jarvises was the Quilter family. Their son, William Quilter, was mentally disabled. In the census he was crudely described as an 'imbecile'. Quilter, when aged 32, was sentenced at Chelmsford Assizes to 20 years' imprisonment for a series of serious sexual assaults on Alice who was only eight years old at the time.[136] One can only imagine as to how this sad tale unfolded, and the arguments and recriminations that took place with their neighbours. This sad story, however, continues. Her mother died the next year. It has not been possible to trace what happened to Alice after this, but two of her three brothers remained in the area, while the remaining brother later moved to London.

William Jarvis died in 1887, a year after Abigail. Sarah remained at the family home until, perhaps through illness or infirmity, she was admitted to the Ongar Union Workhouse at Stanford Rivers where she later died in 1902, aged 86.

Beacon Hill Cottages [47]

The tour continues along Church Road. On the left and running parallel with the road, is the border with Navestock parish. Church Road then branches off to the right. Here on the right was a pair of brick-built, semi-detached cottages with two up, two down, rooms. It is now one dwelling. Owned by the Kelvedon Hall estate and built around 1840-1850, this building was squeezed just inside the parish boundary on a tiny piece of former common land. In fact, if the occupants stepped outside their front door then they were immediately in Navestock parish.

These cottages were occupied by employees of the Kelvedon Hall estate. One of them was occupied for over twenty years by two generations of the Boreham family. John Boreham and his son, Noah Boreham, both served in the British Army. John enlisted in the 23rd Regiment of Light Dragoon Guards at the age of 20 in 1804. He served for nine years in Canada and Ireland, but was discharged as unfit for service 'having received a severe injury to the leg having been kicked by a horse.'[137] Upon his return to the parish of his birth, he worked as an agricultural labourer. His son, Noah Boreham, enlisted in the 51st Regiment of Light infantry in 1839. He served in Australia, India, Ireland and Malta, and attained the rank of sergeant with an exemplary conduct record. Leaving the army in 1860, he returned to the family home, his father having just died. With him was his wife, Mary Ann, whom he had married during his army service, and their children, two of whom had been born abroad in India and Ireland.[138] Both father and son received an army pension; and both must have entertained their fellow parishioners with many tales of their travels and experiences abroad.

Noah Boreham's army experience stood him in good stead because he became a gamekeeper on the Kelvedon Hall estate (until his death in 1871). Landowners and their gamekeepers fought a constant battle to stop poaching, and the challenging job of a gamekeeper often brought them into conflict with other parishioners. The poachers were after pheasants and rabbits, or conies as they were better known as during this period. In the first half of the century, the sentences for poaching were severe and could result in transportation. This meant that a night-time confrontation between a gamekeeper and a gang of poachers, who may have been armed, could often result in violence, especially if the poachers were from another parish and were unknown to the gamekeeper. But most poachers were peaceable, for if they were locals, then they would have been known to the gamekeeper. As the century progressed the system of transportation ceased and poachers could only receive imprisonment or fines. One wonders, however, how fairly they were dealt with at the magistrates' court as almost all of the JPs were owners of extensive estates.

Most Kelvedon Hatch poaching cases involved trespassing in the woodlands of the Kelvedon Hall and Brizes estates trying to catch rabbits using ferrets. Sometimes it was teenage youths such as James Jarvis [46] with two of his friends, John Schooling and Thomas Quilter. Or it was young married men trying to feed their families. One such trio was James Burton, Alfred Burton and Alfred Sawkins who were seen ferretting in woods on the Brizes estate.[139] Each received a fine for their troubles.[140]

Germains Farm [48]

Leaving Beacon Hill Cottages, Church Road now turns into Kelvedon Hall Lane. After descending down a steep hill, a few hundred yards further on is Germains Farm. Germains was a manor in its own right until 1604 when it became part of the Kelvedon Hall estate. The remains of a medieval moat can still be found in its garden. The house itself dates from the sixteenth century with later alterations. In 1920 it was described as a 'picturesque gabled farmhouse, with a rustic porch, drawing room, dining room, kitchen, back kitchen, pantry, dairy, apple store, six bedrooms, a well, and an earth closet.'[141]

Fig. 56. Germains c.1908.

Germains was occupied by various tenant farmers who farmed the 242 acres. From 1870 and until 1886, it was occupied by Robert French. His brother, James, farmed the nearby Langford Bridge Farm [56]. The French family were an old established farming family. Their father, James, had farmed Stondon Hall in neighbouring Stondon Massey. Both Robert and James held important positions in the community as members of the parish vestry and founding members of the school board. The census of April 1871 states that Robert French employed six men and two boys on the farm, but this figure would fluctuate during the year subject to the requirements of the farming year. By 1881, Robert French had moved to another farm in Laindon, Essex, and installed a farm bailiff, James Potter, to oversee Germains Farm.

French tried to respond to the agricultural depression by diversifying and he now included dairy and sheep farming. An auction catalogue shows that he had: 'four fat bullocks, six heifers in milk, six fatting calves, fifty wether sheep (castrated males) and ninety-nine ewes.'[142] But switching to cattle farming brought a new problem: foot and mouth disease. There are several reports of outbreaks of the disease on the farms in Kelvedon Hatch around this time. Another problem arose in 1885 when there was a haystack fire which destroyed the produce of 33 acres. Valued at £100, unfortunately it was not insured.[143] This may well have been a contributory factor in the decision by French to finish the tenancy in September 1886.

The next tenant farmer was William Barr from Fenwick, Ayrshire, in Scotland. So why did Barr leave his farm of 125 acres in Ayrshire and bring his family all the way down to Essex? Barr and a number of other Ayrshire farmers were attracted by advertisements placed in the Scottish newspapers by landowners seeking 'men of energy, intelligence and substance [for] Essex farms within 25 miles of London, at low rents and with freedom of cultivation'.[144] Here the key phrase was freedom of cultivation, and it appealed to the dairy farmers of that area. In order to attract tenants, landowners would make no stipulation on the type of agriculture undertaken on their farms. Many of the dairy farmers brought their cattle with them, some even hiring an entire train to transport the animals. By 1894, there were over 120 families in Essex who were part of this 'Scotch Colony', as it was called, with many living in the Ongar area.[145] Barr, his wife, Annie (who may be the woman in the photograph overleaf dated c.1908), and their ten children, remained living at Germains Farm until his death in 1913 at the age of 90. Their tenancy then finished.

Kelvedon Hall Cottages [49]

Continuing along Kelvedon Hall Lane, on the left was a pair of single storey, semi-detached cottages of an unknown date. Built of brick with a slate roof, these cottages contained four rooms in each. It is now one dwelling. Owned by the Kelvedon Hall estate, they were occupied by various agricultural workers and gamekeepers employed on the estate. In one of them lived William Smith. He lived here for over 40 years with his wife, Fanny. They had two daughters who were both unwell: Fanny was an epileptic and Maria had been lame since her childhood. As well as being an agricultural worker, for over 38 years Smith served as the parish clerk. The duties of the parish clerk were numerous: 'to make responses after the minister during the time of divine service; to give out the psalms proper for the day; to assist the officiating minister in marrying, baptizing, and burying the parishioners, and in all other religious offices and ceremonies of the church.'[146] He was also required to keep the church clean and the churchyard free of weeds. For all this he received £6 a year from the parish vestry.[147]

By 1881, Smith was declining in health and resigned from his office as parish clerk. The rector and the churchwardens, concerned for him and his family's future, launched a subscription for him by a letter to the newspapers: 'he is upwards of 60 years of age and totally un-provided for, and with only, it is feared, the union workhouse before him. He has been of consistent character and much esteemed by all classes for an almost blameless life.'[148] Smith died the following year and the rector wrote another letter of appeal to the newspapers: 'he has left a widow totally un-provided for, and two afflicted daughters'.[149] It is not known how much money was raised by these two appeals, but it seems that it was enough to keep them out of the workhouse. Fanny and her two daughters remained living in the parish in one of the cottages at Old Crown End [43].

Fig. 57.
Harvest time

Fig. 58.
Kelvedon Hall Lodge. (details overleaf)

Part 7

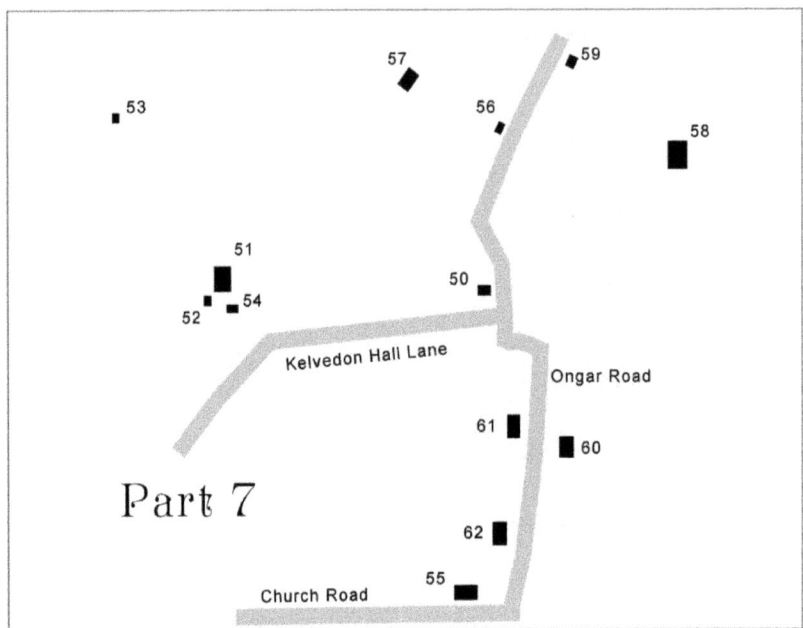

Fig. 59.

Kelvedon Hall Lodge [50] d.

Kelvedon Hall Lane now reaches the junction with Ongar Road. Immediately on the left is the entrance to Kelvedon Hall, the principal manor and largest estate in Kelvedon Hatch, and the second grand mansion on the tour.

At the entrance to the estate was a small picturesque lodge (Fig. 58). Built c.1839, the lodge provided accommodation for estate workers and servants who also acted as the gatekeepers. The lodge had become uninhabitable by 1920. It was demolished and replaced in 1938.

Occupants of the Lodge included William Fenner who served as coachman to the Wright family for at least 12 years (1871-1882). Another long-term occupier was John Archer. He is described on the census returns as an agricultural labourer, but he was probably a gardener on the estate. He and his wife, Olivia, lived in the lodge for over 32 years (c.1841-1873). In 1845, two local labourers broke into the lodge and stole two silver watches and six shillings in cash belonging to Archer. They were both arrested and sentenced to ten years' transportation.[150]

Kelvedon Hall [51]

A short carriage drive through an avenue of trees leads up to Kelvedon Hall and the Church of St Nicholas. The manor of Kelvedon Hall appears in the Domesday Book. In 1538, the manor was purchased by John Wright. For the next eleven generations, with one exception mentioned below, the estate passed from father to eldest son – and each of them named John. Quite remarkable when one considers infant mortality rates in previous centuries. The family had been Roman Catholics since 1605, and despite difficult times when Catholics were persecuted and their civil rights severely curtailed, they had managed to retain the estate.

The present house was built c.1742, replacing a Tudor house. A detailed description of the property appears in a letting advertisement from 1865:

'Capital Mansion distinguished as Kelvedon Hall, approached by a carriage drive from a lodge entrance through a fine avenue, and seated in a beautifully timbered park ....The accommodation comprises, on the upper floors, 13 principal and secondary bed-chambers, dressing-rooms, and boudoirs; on the ground floor, noble entrance hall; dining-room; drawing-room; library; breakfast-room; and gun-room. The domestic offices comprise, in the east wing, kitchen scullery, butler's and housekeeper's apartments, with servants' bedrooms over; in the east wing, capital laundry, brewhouse and dairy, game and meat larders, etc., with excellent arched vaults for wine and beer under the mansion; enclosed carriage yard, with standing for four carriages, stabling for 12 horses, and loose boxes, harness-rom, granary, lofts, etc.; warm farm-yard, with range of excellent buildings. The pleasure grounds and gardens are laid out with great taste in lawns, flower-beds and adorned with clumps of evergreens and shrubs and a fine sheet of water stored with fish; walled kitchen gardens sloping to the south, fully cropped and planted with choice fruit trees, vinery green-house, melon-ground, etc., - the whole about 12 acres. There is an abundance of game. The entire property is well supplied with excellent water, and is within easy distance of two foxhounds. There is a private chapel, with vestry adjoining, attached to the mansion, and they would be let with the premises if taken by a Catholic tenant.'[151]

Within the parish boundaries, the estate consisted of four farms, several houses and cottages; and 800 acres of pasture, arable land, and woods. The Wright family also owned the manor of White Notley, Essex, and White Notley Hall, the manor house.

In 1837, John Francis Wright, at the age of 21 and having attained his majority, took possession of the estate from his grandfather's trustees, his own father having died in 1822 and his grandfather in 1826.

To celebrate attaining the estate, he donated coals and blankets to the poor of the parish. This was the first of many charitable donations he made to the parishioners during his life. Every Christmas he gave two fatted bullocks - enough to feed 100 people - together with blankets, warm clothing and coals. Soup was also given to the poor during the winter months. Because of his paternal attitude to his parishioners, the newspapers often described him as like the 'old English gentlemen, full of benevolence'. Wright served as a JP and was High Sheriff for Essex in 1857. He also involved himself in many local associations such as the Ongar Labourers' Friend Society. Like his ancestors, Wright was a conscientious Roman Catholic, and the principal house servants were also Catholics. The arrangements for his domestic servants were unusual for a Victorian household. His butler, James Clarkson, married Susanna Bouldron in 1842, and she went on to become the housekeeper. Other relations of theirs took up other roles in the household. His nephews were footmen, while her sister and niece worked as housemaid and laundry-maid. All of the servants were originally from Yorkshire. Wright's mother and grandmother were both from families with large Yorkshire estates, so it is probable that these servants were found through this connection. After Wright's death, Clarkson and his wife retired and lived at Mushroom Hall [3].

Wright never married, so when he died in 1865, the John Wright line came to an end. Despite the outward appearances of wealth, for the last years of his life he had financial problems. In 1840, the bank of Wright & Co., of London was declared bankrupt (there may have been a family connection, albeit several generations earlier).[152] The bank was well-known for having numerous Catholics as its clients, including the Duke of Norfolk and the 11th Lord Petre of Ingatestone Hall, Essex. It is believed that Wright suffered substantial losses in the bank's collapse and had to seek a mortgage of £7,000 from the Duke of Norfolk. In his will, Wright appointed trustees to administer the mortgage and estate after his death. Following careful financial management, the mortgage was repaid before 1920.

After Wright's death, the estate passed to his fifteen-year-old nephew, Edward Carington Wright. Carington Wright did not take up immediate occupancy because of his age. Instead, the property was let out to a tenant, Captain John Ellis. Ellis is an interesting character. After a short career in the Royal Navy, he became a tea merchant in Singapore and made a small fortune. His hobby was languages and he could speak eleven fluently, including three Chinese dialects. Ellis then moved to Australia and made an even larger fortune in farming. He then returned home to England to live the life of a gentleman. He stayed at Kelvedon Hall for only a few years, by 1871 he had moved to Kempton Park in Surrey.[153] Interestingly, some servants from Kelvedon Hatch went with him: Walter Roast, a stable boy, and two young female servants by the name of Wallis who were the daughters of a former coachman to John Francis Wright.

Edward Carington Wright now moved into Kelvedon Hall. In 1873, he married Mary Julia Petre, second daughter of Henry Petre, of Springfield, the second son of the 11th Lord Petre. Carington Wright followed in the footsteps of his uncle by making annual gifts to the poor of the village (although these seem to cease after 1875, perhaps because of the increasingly militant attitude of the agricultural workers). He also involved himself in local affairs: he was founder member of the school board [10]; supporter of the Catholic church in Ongar; and member of the Essex Chamber of Agriculture and Essex Agriculture Society. As important members of the local Catholic community, he and his wife were honoured with a visit by Cardinal Archbishop Manning.[154]

He became a JP in 1879, but this was put in jeopardy by a confrontation with the local rector, the Revd Samuel Slocock, in 1884. The resulting court case generated great interest in the area, and on the day of the hearing, the Ongar magistrates' court was crowded. Carington Wright was charged with unlawfully and maliciously killing a dog belonging to Slocock. Another dog was also shot, but this charge was not proceeded with. Two facts were agreed: the dogs were often found wandering in the grounds of Kelvedon Hall and Slocock had previously been warned that they may be shot; and secondly, that Carington Wright had shot them. Why they were shot on that day and what the dogs were doing at the time was never answered as Carington Wright did not go into the witness box. He was found guilty and fined five guineas, and he had to pay two guineas compensation for the dog.[155] No record has been found of Carington Wright sitting as a JP after this court case, although he did keep the title.

The family's life and their status in the community was also about to change for another reason. The couple had one daughter, Beatrice, who had been born soon after their marriage. In 1886, Carington Wright started an affair with the child's governess, Mary Knowles, aged 23. The full story is not known, but in 1887, Knowles gave birth to a daughter, and in the following year, she had a son. It would seem that Carington Wright then went to Madeira for three months. His wife is not mentioned in the 1891 census, so perhaps she also went abroad to avoid the scandal. Carington Wright next appears in the 1891 census for Tunbridge Wells in the same house as Knowles where he is described as a visitor. The couple then moved to the south coast where they then lived together and had another child in 1896. His wife died in 1908, and now he was free to marry Knowles, which he did in the same year. Carington Wright died in 1920.

Fig. 60. Kelvedon Hall c.1910.

In August 1891, Carington Wright left Kelvedon Hall for good and the house was let to a tenant: John Algernon Jones, a wealthy city stockbroker. He lived here with his wife, Gertrude, and their six daughters and one son, John (better known as Bertram). The photograph (Fig. 60) may be of Jones, fishing on the lake which lies in front of the hall. There are more photographs of the family from this time and they appear in Figs. 61 - 65.

Jones engaged with the parish community and was supportive of the building of the new church, and provided money for the parish room [14]. During the First World War, part of the Hall was given over to convalescing soldiers. Jones died in 1916. Gertrude remained living in the Hall and purchased it in 1922 when the estate was broken up by Carington Wright's nephew and heir, Sir Henry J Lawson. After her death, her son, Betram, sold the Hall and moved to the former rectory [60], which by then had been replaced by a new rectory built next to the new church.

Fig. 61. Jones shortly before he took up the tenancy of Kelvedon Hall.

Fig. 62 and 63. Scenes at Kelvedon Hall.

At the front door of Kelvedon Hall. In the centre are John Algernon Jones and his wife, Gertrude. On the right is one of his daughters. The identity of the man is not known. Jones was noted for having several peacocks wandering the grounds.

Figs. 64 and 65. Carriages kept at Kelvedon Hall during the time of the Joneses.

One villager recalled seeing carriages arriving at church for the morning service: 'You would see a 'carriage and pair' coming along, probably from Kelvedon Hall; a 'brougham and single' from Mr Royd's perhaps, and others; and of course the farmers would come along with ponies and tub-carts.'[156]

Gardener's Cottage [52] d.

Attached to the north side of the kitchen-garden wall was a small gardener's cottage. A window was made in the kitchen-garden wall which allowed the gardener to overlook the garden – probably to look out for rabbits eating the plants. For at least 30 years the cottage was occupied by George Bodgby and his wife, Sarah. Hard work and fresh air clearly did him no harm; he died at the age of 90 in 1879. The next gardener was William Hobby. Originally from Dorset, he lived here with his wife, Clara, and their eight children (and also in Kelvedon Hall Cottages [49]). Well known in the parish, he supported the church, and became a member of the parish council and school board. In 1908, his son, Charles, and his wife, Rose, emigrated to Canada. Perhaps encouraged by good news from his son, five years later, William and Clara followed them. By 1921, both families lived in small log cabins on a small acreage of land in Saskatchewan.

Gamekeeper's Cottage [53] *d.*

Beyond Kelvedon Hall and near Park Wood was a collection of farm buildings and a small cottage. No description of it survives. This served as the gamekeeper's cottage. For almost 40 years, William Sitch was employed on the estate as gamekeeper; and for some of this time he lived here with his wife, Ann, and their four children. Living here must have been a challenge for them as the nearest fresh water was several hundred yards away at the main house. Perhaps this is why the cottage does not appear in the records after his death in 1885.

Old St Nicholas' Church [54]

Fig. 66. The old church.

Fig. 67. The old church c.1893.

Next to Kelvedon Hall was St Nicholas' Church. The Georgian-style church was built in 1753 to replace a medieval church which had fallen into disrepair. According to the curate at the time: 'by reason of the negligence of the parishioners as to be utterly unfit for the performance of Divine Service there, with either safety or decency.'[157] The new church had Venetian-style windows, and contained a west-gallery, high square pews, and a three-tiered pulpit. The photograph in Fig. 66 dates from the 1880s, while the above photograph (Fig. 67) is from c.1893.

The advowson (the right to present a clergyman to the living when it next became vacant) was held by a patron. In the case of Kelvedon Hatch, the advowson at first descended with the manor of Kelvedon Hall, but in the seventeenth century when the Wrights became Roman Catholics, they lost the right to present the rector. The advowson had a financial value and could be bought and sold. There are reports of it being auctioned in 1826, 1842 and 1859, and between 1842 and 1889 it rose in price from £1,510 to £3,450.[158] The living at Kelvedon Hatch consisted of the rectory house [60] and 27 acres of glebe land, and the great and small tithes (commuted to a monetary value).

Once a rector was appointed it did not always mean they would officiate in the church and live in the rectory. Sometimes the rector lived elsewhere as they had commitments to another parish. In their absence, there was a curate to conduct services. This was the case with the Revd John Bannister, rector from 1832 until 1870. He was also the Perpetual Curate and later Vicar of

West Worldham, Hampshire. However, he did reside in the rectory for eleven years from 1845 to 1856 with his wife, Matilda, and son, William, who was also a church minister. Despite being absent from the parish for some of the time, he provided funds for a school for the children of the parish [10].

After Bannister's death in 1870, the Revd Slocock (Fig. 68) became rector. Slocock's father had purchased the advowson a few years earlier and bequeathed it to him in his will.[159] Slocock, unlike Bannister, remained in the parish throughout his time as rector. He lived in the rectory with his wife, Mary, and their two sons and two daughters. Slocock was a founder member of the school board [10], and judging by the many letters he wrote to the newspapers, he had a genuine concern for his parishioners, particularly the poorest among them. Soon

Fig. 68 Revd Slocock.

after he became rector, he set about much-needed renovations to the fabric of the church building which was described as 'the most dilapidated and neglected in the diocese'. This was probably because of the often absent Revd Bannister. The renovation cost £380 and was paid for by voluntary subscriptions. Alterations included the removal of the gallery and the three-tiered pulpit; and installation of underfloor heating, new choir seats and pews; and a lectern and pulpit.[160] It is clear from the newspaper articles that Slocock and other churchmen immensely disliked the Georgian architecture of the church building. Thirteen years later, urgent repairs were required to the church, this time to keep it watertight. More money was needed to pay for a new oak steeple and new roof, and for the painting and colouring of the interior of the church. This time voluntary subscriptions raised £300.[161] The church reopened in July 1887 with a celebratory service.

Slocock knew that for some parishioners attending church required a walk of nearly five miles, there and back. Many of them made the trip three times on a Sunday. In winter, the walk could be even more challenging with mud and bad weather deterring even the most fervent worshipper. He was also aware that the Wesleyan Chapel [15] was far more conveniently located on the former common. His answer to this was to arrange regular evening services in the new schoolroom [10]. This was so successful that the next rector also used the schoolroom for services and other church events. The remoteness of this church was part of the reason a new church came to be built near to the former common. After the new church was built, the old church was no longer used. Too expensive to maintain, it was later deconsecrated. It then gradually fell into ruins and was partly demolished.

New St Nicholas' Church [55]

In 1889, Slocock resigned his living. His wife, Mary, had died in 1887, and now for personal reasons he considered that it was time to move to a new parish at West Rounton in Yorkshire. He died there in 1901. Slocock sold the advowson to Edward William Puxon, a stockbroker. Puxon presented the living to his son-in-law, the Revd David Wilkie Peregrine, who, with his wife, Constance, then moved into the rectory [60]. They were to have two sons and three daughters while living there.

Peregrine (Fig. 69) was full of enthusiasm for his new role. He was one of the more evangelical clergy in the Church of England during the late-Victorian period. It was during his time that the temperance movement was active and well supported in Kelvedon Hatch. Soon after Peregrine's arrival, he and the churchwardens faced a problem: the churchyard was full and it was soon to be closed by the Home Office. According to new local government regulations, the parish would be required to open a new burial ground

Fig. 69
Revd Peregrine.

and build a chapel of ease - as well as having to maintain the parish church. The first problem was to find a suitable piece of land. Fortunately, the Revd Charles Leopold Royds, owner of the Brizes estate [28], offered to grant a plot of land for a burial ground providing a church would be built on the site. Peregrine recognised that this was a good opportunity to bring the church building closer to the more densely populated part of the parish. He and the church wardens accepted the land offered by Royds. Peregrine was also fortunate to have living in the village the architect John Thomas Newman [42] who agreed to give his architectural services for free.

In early 1893, an energetic fund-raising campaign was launched. The target was £2000, a large sum for a parish in the middle of an agricultural depression. Not only that, a parallel fund-raising effort to build a working men's club and parish room was also launched. Money was raised through voluntary subscriptions, rummage sales, fetes, and pound sales where items weighing a pound were sold for £1. By September 1893, sufficient money was raised to enable the start of construction. On 30 October 1894, at a special church service held in the pouring rain, the memorial stone was laid with a new three-penny piece placed beneath it. By then, £1,600 had been raised. The church was finally completed and consecrated on 1 November 1895.[162] (Fig. 70)

The church is a good example of the Arts and Crafts Movement with brickwork on show, elaborate wrought-iron work (donated by the Puxon family), and an impressive oak hammer-beam roof. There is some continuity with the past: the pews from the old church were moved to the new church,

Fig. 70. The new church in 1895.

as were the medieval font and the bell. (Later in the twentieth century, brass memorials and glass from the altar window of the old church were also transferred to the new church.) Two gospel lights were purchased with money donated by 'natives of West Africa'. The money came via the Revd Peregrine's brother who was a District Commissioner with the Colonial Civil Service in what is now Ghana. The communion rails were purchased with money raised at the Queen Victoria's diamond jubilee celebrations held in the parish in 1897.

During the following months, the enthusiasm surrounding the opening of the new church was tinged with sadness when there were the deaths of three people connected with the building of the church: John Newman, the architect; the Revd Royds, who donated the land; and Edward Puxon, the patron.

Peregrine remained in the parish until 1905, when he then exchanged livings with the Revd Laurence Rayner Tuttiett from Branston in Lincolnshire. It is not known why Peregrine wished to leave the parish. Tuttiett did not remain for long in the parish. He was replaced in 1908 by the Revd William Samuel Mavor, who, as revealed in the story of the parish room [15], had a high-handed manner and was not popular with everyone in the parish.

Fig. 71. The new church under construction.

Fig. 72. Builders of the church.
The building firm of John Gozzett of Maldon were awarded the contract after they had submitted the successful tender.

Langford Bridge Farm [56]

Leaving the Kelvedon Hall estate, the route re-joins the Ongar Road and continues north until on the left is Langford Bridge Cottages and Langford Bridge Farm. The name Langford Bridge refers to the nearby bridge which crosses the River Roding. The name Langford was first recorded in 1582[163] and was probably named after a local landowner on the Ongar side of the river.

An earlier farm of the same name stood some 400 metres to the east of its present location. In 1778, the owners of Kelvedon Hall [51] and Great Myles [58] agreed that the farm should be moved to its present site and the Ongar road re-routed. The reason stated was to improve the road for travellers by removing two sharp bends, but it is thought that the real reason for the change was to allow the occupants of Great Myles to have a more delightful prospect across their parkland and lake. The old farm was demolished soon after the agreement and the new farm built.

Owned by the Kelvedon Hall estate, in 1881 Langford Bridge Farm consisted of 175 acres of mainly pasture. The farm buildings were improved and added to during the nineteenth century - only for a barn, stable and cowhouse to be destroyed by fire in 1909[164]. In 1920 the farm house was described as consisting of a 'hall, dining room, drawing room, kitchen, scullery, dairy, wash-house, cellar, eight bedrooms', with the outside facilities of a 'well and an earth closet'.[165] Like the farmers at the adjacent Germains Farm, the farmers of Langford Bridge tried to adapt to the agricultural depression by changing their farming to cattle, cows and milk production. But they still struggled. In 1885, after 25 years' tenancy, James French could not pay his rent and was forced to sell his farm equipment to pay his rent arrears. He then quit the farm.[166]

The next tenant, Edward Dodgson, was a farmer from Kirkby Lonsdale, Westmorland. Like the Scottish farmers, he travelled south to take advantage of the 'freedom of cultivation'. But after twelve years of hard work his dreams were shattered when he found he could not pay the rent. Like James French before him, he was forced to sell his farm equipment to pay the rent arrears.[167] Dodgson left the farm in 1897 and returned to Westmorland.

Following Dodgson was Isaiah Hobson Mugleston. He was more successful. With his wife, Louise, and their eleven children, he lived at the farm for almost 25 years. Mugleston had previously been the tenant farmer at Grays Farm in High Ongar, and he continued farming there after his move to Langford Bridge Farm. He also took over farming the acres at Hatch Farm [13]. Meanwhile, Louise had a talent for water divining by using a hazel twig, and the 1901 census returns shows her occupation as such. When the Church House [14] was established, she was asked to find out if there was any water underground so that a well could be dug. Her two daughters, May and Gertrude, inherited her talents and were also accomplished water diviners. All three were called upon by farmers seeking underground springs on their fields, and sometimes even local authorities would employ their services.[168]

Langford Bridge Cottages [57]

This pair of brick-built, semi-detached cottages were built in the last two decades of the nineteenth century and occupied by agricultural workers. In 1900, one of them was occupied by George Clarke and his family. Clarke had previously worked as a cowman on Mugleston's farm in High Ongar and had followed him to Kelvedon Hatch. These cottages were the scene of the only known case of murder in the parish. Clarke's wife was named Mary Ann, and they had four children. The youngest was Tiny Margaret Clarke, aged 3 years 11 months (and yes, Tiny was her first name). There is no evidence about the mother's prior mental condition, but one day while her husband was at work, she slashed the poor child's neck with a razor and tried to do the same to her eldest son, George, aged 13. She then tried to cut her own throat. At her trial, she was declared insane at the time of the murder and was sentenced to be detained at Her Majesty's Pleasure. It is not known what became of her.[169] George, meanwhile, remained at Langford Bridge Cottages with his children for at least another ten years.

Great Myles [58] *part d.*

Continuing north along the Ongar Road, just before Langford Bridge is a lodge house and the entrance to what was the third grand mansion in the parish: Great Myles. A manor in its own right, it appears in the Domesday Book. In 1566, the manor was acquired by the Luther family and descended with them until it passed by marriage to Henry Fane. The Fanes were an ancient family and Henry's eldest brother was the 8th Earl of Westmorland. There is no surviving detailed description of the house and only two pictures of it are known. Built in the sixteenth century, it was enlarged in 1701. It was said to have a window for every day of the year. This may be an exaggeration, but as can be seen from the diagram of the front and side of the house based on a print and the tithe map (Fig. 73), it certainly had a large number of windows.[170]

Fig. 73. Great Myles (diagram)

By the 1820s, the property was held by John Fane, M.P. for Oxfordshire. After a failed attempt to sell the property,[171] the house was leased out to tenants who included Richard Chetwynd, 6th Viscount Chetwynd of Bearhaven (1831); and Alexander Gordon, son of Charles Gordon of Cluny who held extensive estates in Scotland (1837). In 1842, a further attempt was made to sell the mansion and estate. A description of the property appeared in the Times newspaper:

> 'Highly important and distinguished property, well known as Great Myless, consisting of mansion, park and woodlands, to which may be added the exclusive right of shooting over upwards of 2,600 acres. The mansion is delightfully situate, on an eminence, environed with shrubberies, gardens, plantations, and fine sheet of water in the foreground; its arrangements are complete for a family of distinction. The detached offices are of an extensive and superior character, comprising stabling for 22 horse, five carriage-houses, and other buildings of corresponding extent. The park is finely timbered and belted, and extends to 75 acres; its ornamental lake is crossed near the centre by the bridge. The woodlands are of a superior order, not rivalled in the whole count for the production of oak, and comprises about 50 acres.' [172]

The property was not sold, so in a foretaste of what would become the fate of many great mansions in the twentieth century, a decision was made to demolish the mansion.[173] All that remained was the service wing, a stable block and outbuildings. The former service wing was then converted into two dwellings, and then later, into one. During the rest of the century they were occupied by various agricultural workers and remained in the ownership of the Fane family.

Great Myles Lodge [59]

Standing at the entrance to Great Myles was a lodge. A small, two-roomed property probably built at the end of the eighteenth century. It was occupied for over forty years by the Harvey family (1871-1911). William Harvey, a labourer, was a single man and lived here with his widowed mother. After her death, he married a widower, Mary Sitch, who moved in with her two sons. They then had at least six children. Their sons left school at the age of 12 and obtained employment milking cows and bird scaring. They were still living at home and employed as cowmen some ten years later.

While in this part of the parish, this will be an opportunity to look at the subject of railways. During the Victorian period, on two occasions plans were laid before Parliament proposing construction of new railways which would have crossed the parish. Neither came to fruition. The first was the Essex Midland Junction Railway in 1848. The proposal was to connect the

Eastern Counties Railway with the North Eastern Counties Railway. The proposed route ran through Harlow, Greensted, Stondon Massey, across part of the Great Myles estate, and on to Shenfield.[174] Ten years later, the other proposed scheme was for a London, Dunmow, Clare and Bury St. Edmunds Railway. The local route ran from Ilford to Ongar following the valley of the River Roding, passing through Kelvedon Hatch parish on the west side and across the Kelvedon Hall estate.[175] This scheme lost out to the extension of the Eastern Counties' railway line from Loughton to Ongar. In 1891, many of the farmers and landowners in Kelvedon Hatch and Doddinghurst raised a petition seeking extension of this railway through their parishes to Shenfield, but it was unsuccessful.

Rectory [60]

Retracing the route along the Ongar Road and past the entrance to Kelvedon Hall, on the left is the former Rectory, now split into two properties known as Old Kelvedon Grange and Kelvedon Grange. The land on which the house stands is mentioned in a grant of land dated 1344, and part of the building dates from the sixteenth century, with eighteenth and nineteenth-century alterations and additions. Adjacent to the house were a number of buildings including a tithe barn, stables and other farm buildings. These were demolished in 1879, and replaced by a new stable, coach-house and outbuildings.[176] Surrounding the rectory were gardens, an orchard and 27 acres of glebe land. The history of the house is well documented because it is associated with the church. From 1610 until 1931, the house was mainly occupied by the various rectors and curates who were the incumbents or ministers for St Nicholas' Church. The occupants for the period 1840 – 1920 were:

 1840-1841 Revd Henry Landon, curate
 1841-1845 Revd James Barry, curate
 1845-1856 Revd John Bannister, rector
 1856-1866 Revd George Raynor, curate
 1866-1870 Revd George Lucas Moore, curate
 1870-1889 Revd Samuel Slocock, rector
 1889-1905 Revd David Peregrine, rector
 1905-1908 Revd Laurence Rayner Tuttiett, rector
 1908-1927 Revd William Samuel Mavor, rector

During the time of Slocock and Peregrine, the rectory gardens were often the venue for social and fund-raising events such as garden parties, temperance meetings, and teas for the church choir and Sunday school.

Fig. 74. The Rectory c.1893.

Fig. 75. Revd Slocock in front of the Rectory c.1885.

Pump House Farm [61]

Opposite the Rectory is Pump House Farm. Built in the seventeenth century with later alterations and additions, it is a timber–framed 'u' shaped house. Owned by the Kelvedon Hall estate it contained two sitting rooms, kitchen, larder, five bedrooms, while outside there was a brewhouse, coalhouse, well, earth closet, and wide range of farm buildings.[177] It was occupied by various tenant farmers who farmed the arable fields which ranged in acreage from 155 to 183 acres. From c.1860 until 1883, the farm was occupied by George Littlechild, his wife, Sarah, and their nine children. They were part of a larger Littlechild family who also were tenant farmers in Doddinghurst and Stondon Massey. At one time, Littlechild was also the tenant of the windmill on the common [1]. Like his fellow farmers in the parish, Littlechild struggled to make farming profitable and to pay his rent. In 1883 he quit his tenancy and left the farm.

While living at the farm, Littlechild was the victim of an attempted robbery and became a celebrated figure for his bravery. On the night of 22 March 1879, Littlechild was returning home from Ongar railway station with his fourteen-year-old son, George. As he walked through Marden Ash he noticed a group of men hanging around. The men then walked off. Littlechild's suspicions, however, were raised; he armed himself with his pocket knife and tied his purse around his ankle. Continuing their journey in the darkness, as they approached Langford Bridge he was pounced upon and knocked to the ground. As the assailants were rifling through his pockets, he defended himself by stabbing one of the men in the neck. All the assailants ran off except one, a William Flack, who Littlechild managed to restrain by the threat of further violence with the knife should he resist. His son ran and called for the help of William Harvey at Great Myles Lodge [59] (who, we learn from the newspaper report, was nicknamed 'Bullace'). Together they took Flack to the Ongar Police Station. Police later traced one accomplice: George Benton. On examination he was found to be covered in blood and had two large cuts to his neck. In court, Flack's defence was that he was sleep-walking! Both men were sentenced to 18 months' hard labour.[178] The case caused much excitement in the area, and on Romford Market a public subscription was raised among the farmers and presented to Littlechild. Someone even wrote a poem about his bravery: *Littlechild or the modern St George*.[179]

The next tenant was Frank Coleman (Fig. 76). He was from a farming family; his father had farmed Bois Hall in Navestock for at least eleven years. Coleman married a Navestock farmer's daughter, Martha Miles, in 1883, and then took up the tenancy of Pump House Farm. They had seven children while they were living at the farm. Coleman immediately involved himself in parish activities: he was churchwarden for eighteen years and was one of the

Fig. 76. Coleman family.

driving forces behind the raising of funds for the new church. He also acted as a trustee of the parish charities. The Coleman family remained at the farm until 1902. They then decided to emigrate to Canada to seek new opportunities. The family travelled to Saskatchewan where they were again engaged in farming.

Priors [62]

A little further along the Ongar Road was Priors, a former farm house which was now a gentleman's residence. The proportional red brick Georgian façade hides an earlier seventeenth-century timber-frame. The house, the farm buildings opposite, and land consisting of 31 acres, were part of the Great Myles's estate and owned by the Fane family [58].

The house was let to the Revd John Alder, curate at Stanford Rivers, from 1840 to 1846. The next known occupant is the Revd Frederick Adrian Scrope Fane who lived here from 1851 until his death in 1894. Fane was the brother of John Fane who held Great Myles. At first he was the curate at Magdalen Laver, and then in 1855, he became the rector of the tiny parish of Norton Mandeville. This parish did not have a rectory, so Fane lived at Priors. The parish was also poor, so it was fortunate that Fane came from a wealthy family and was financially secure. Fane had married Joanna Hobhouse, youngest daughter of Sir Benjamin Hobhouse, 1st Baronet of Hobhouse, and they had five children. On the census returns the household is shown with a full complement of servants including a children's governess. The Revd Fane was a local character. He was a typical mid-Victorian country clergyman involved in local government organisations and many local philanthropic associations involved in helping the poor. He was chairman of the Ongar Union Board of Guardians for 27 years, and a member of the Ongar Rural District Council. He was also a keen foxhunter, rider and cricketer (a skill which his grandson inherited, reaching the achievement of playing for England).

He was also a brave man. On 13 January 1882, at four o'clock in the morning, Fane was awoken by a fire already well alight in the stables next to the house. William Wingar, the coachman, was sleeping in a room above the stables. With tiles and burning rafters falling around him, and in his bare feet, Fane tried on at least three occasions to fight through the flames and enter the stables, but he was unable to rescue Wingar who died in the fire. The stables were also burnt to the ground. At the inquest held in the Eagle Inn [24], Fane regretted that he was unable to do more. However, he was assured by the coroner that he had done all that he could and it was likely that Wingar had died before Fane made his rescue attempts. Fane replied: 'I only did my duty. I only wish I could have done more, and I would if I had the time over again.' [180]

After Fane's death in 1894 at the age of 84, Priors was occupied by his son, Colonel Frederick John Fane, who by this time had retired from military service. His military experience, however, was called upon during World War One when he was appointed military representative of the Local Committee of the Defence of the Realm which was formed in the event of a German invasion. He also served on the parish council.

Caravan [63] *d.*

Returning now to somewhere on the former common land, and the last stop on this part of the tour. It is a tinker's caravan. For over 23 years, from at least 1861 to 1884, Benjamin Fletcher, cutler and tin plate worker, lived at the roadside in a caravan which also served as his workshop. A widower and elderly, he died at the age of 79 in 1884.

The sight of caravans on the roadside, and itinerant traders, drovers, gypsies and tramps wandering the roads, would not have been unusual, but they all would have been treated with the greatest suspicion.

Fig. 77. Snow on Boxing Day 1906.

Overnight there had been a snow storm which left snow up to the depth of eight inches in places. This view is on the Ongar Road looking north-east towards the church [55]. On the left is the parish room [15]. The trees by the figure are still there.

Fig. 78. The windmill.
Eliza Purkis and a child pose in front of the windmill.
To the right is the beginning of Mill Lane.

Part 8

Doddinghurst

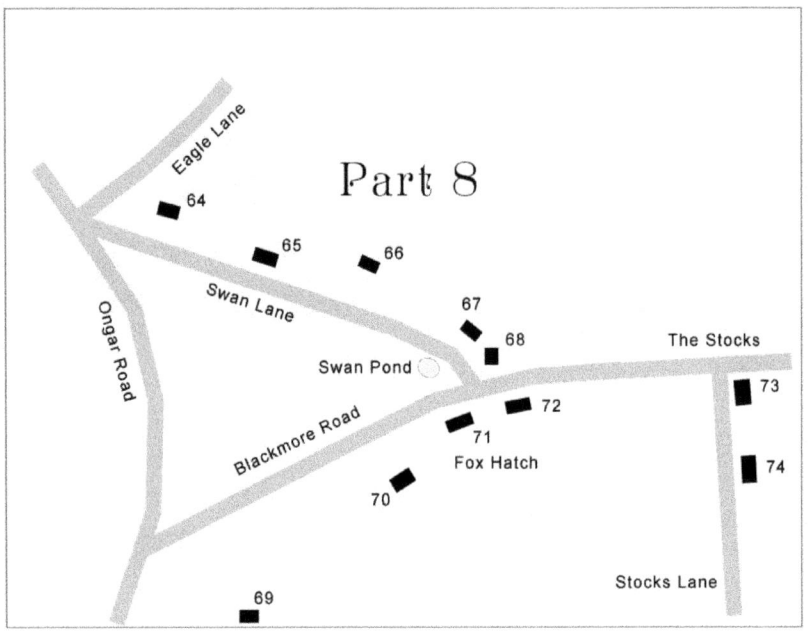

Fig. 79.

The tour now moves to the other side of the common, which at the time came under Doddinghurst parish. As mentioned earlier, in the late-twentieth century the parish boundaries were changed with Kelvedon Hatch parish taking over part of Doddinghurst parish. This tour only includes the properties in the Fox Hatch/Swan Pond area.

Doddinghurst parish was administered by its own parish vestry, and later, by a parish council, but these will not be described any further. By 1840, all the properties surrounding the common were either held copyhold of the manor of Doddinghurst Hall, or were freehold (many of them owned by the Brizes estate [28]). Doddinghurst Hall was owned by the Fane family, who were previously discussed under Great Myles [58], and later by the Shaw family.

Fig. 80. Swan Lane from the Ongar Road c.1910.
On the left is part of Harley Cottages [64]; in the distance is the baker's [65] and the Stores [72].

School / Harley Cottages [64] d.

This part of the tour starts in Swan Lane which led from the Ongar Road to Swan Pond. On the left and at some distance back off the lane was a plot of land. The first known building on this site was a timber house. It was used as the school [10] for at least ten years or more (1841-1851). It was owned by William Cooper, who lived opposite [25]. In 1850 he sold the house to Louisa Dolby of Brizes [28]. Some years later, the timber house was demolished and replaced by a pair of brick-built, semi-detached cottages. Known as Harley Cottages, they were occupied by workers on the Brizes estate who included John Sherry and Thomas Peagram, who were both gardeners. Harley Cottages was later surrounded by a modern housing estate and became part of the road called Finchingfields.

Cottage [65]

A little further along Swan Lane is the property now known as Ivy Cottage. In May 1836, James Nottage, a painter and glazier, was granted permission to enclose a small part of the common. Within two years he had built the cottage and sold it to Dinah and Sarah Westley, spinsters. The house also had a shop to the side of it. The Westleys became the shopkeepers, and they let part of the house to a carpenter, and then to a hay-binder's family. After their time in the property, ownership of the property passed down their family line and was let out to tenants. It was later acquired by the Brizes estate.

Fig. 81 Herbert Curtis outside his house c.1890. Note the shop on the right.

William Smith was the first tenant, and after his death, the shopkeeper's role passed to his son, Edward (1861 to 1887). The next tenant was Herbert Curtis (Fig. 81). Curtis lived here with his wife, Martha, and their children. The shop was now also a bakery and the property was described as 'brick-built and slated...containing eight rooms, with a front shop, bakehouse, three bushel oven, stable, cart shed, hay shed, large garden and yard.' [181]

In July 1893, Herbert Curtis was a witness at the wedding of Elizabeth Babb and Charles Brown at Doddinghurst Church. The wedding celebrations, which took place somewhere near here, were apparently a little lively judging by a letter of complaint which appeared in the Kelvedon Hatch parish magazine. The complaint was about 'rough music'. Before setting out the letter, a little explanation about rough music is needed. Rough music was a working-class custom which had its origins in medieval times. By the early-nineteenth century, it had become a wedding ritual as much as our modern-day stag and hen parties. Youths and young men of the parish would arrive at a wedding feast armed with kettles, pots and pans, shovels and meat cleavers. They would boisterously bang these together trying to make some sort of tune, but invariably created such a noise that it 'would fright the living and raise the dead'. Then after wishing the couple much happiness, if they were lucky, they would be given beer and perhaps money by the bridegroom. Over the years it eventually turned into a form of blackmail. If they were not rewarded for their music, then the noise would continue unabated. Sometimes things got out of hand, windows were smashed and it could even turn violent with the wedding guests becoming involved in a brawl with the musicians. By the end of the nineteenth century, the police were under strict orders to stamp out rough music. This is the letter (the date of the letter, and the location and the circumstances described can only match the wedding of Babb and Brown):

> 'Are we living far away from civilisation, in the centre of the dark Continent, or in civilised and peaceful England? It should seem the former, judging from the heathenish noise that took place on Kelvedon Common one night some weeks back. And what was it all about? A certain young man was deluded enough to take unto himself a wife. Some of his friends wished, we presume, to show their disapproval of being robbed of the chances of gaining the affections of the said woman, showed their jealousy by indulging in what is commonly called Rough Music. Now, sir, if such a thing had taken place among the wild and heathen tribes under English rule, it would have been suppressed at once with the greatest rigour. Why is such a state of things allowed in Essex? It is nothing more or less than a scandal, that peaceable citizens should be disturbed; and a disgrace to all who took part in it. If this noisy crew wish to drink the bride and groom's health, why they did not so like men, and subscribe for it among themselves, instead of afterwards trying to extort it at other people's expense. Rough Music after weddings has long since been given up in other villages, let us hope that Kelvedon Hatch will follow their example.
>
> Signed, Anon.'[182]

The Curtis family moved out of the house in the mid-1900s and into one of the cottages in The Thorns [31]. Interestingly, in the 1911 census Curtis is described as an unemployed baker. It is not clear whether this was permanent or temporary unemployment. Meanwhile, Martha was employed as a cook in the Rectory [60]. Martha died in 1912, and Hebert and his family later moved into Mill Villa [2].

Cottage [66]

Continuing along Swan Lane, on the left is a timber-framed property dating from c.1700, with later additions. It is now known as The Forge. As the name suggests, this was occupied by a blacksmith and wheelwright. For 49 years until 1913, George Godfrey and his wife, Selina, lived here. The smithy was located both here and in some buildings a few yards further down the lane next to the Swan Inn.

Swan Inn [67]

The lane now reaches Swan Pond and the Swan Inn (the building is now an Indian restaurant). For centuries, Swan Pond was a stopping-off point for drovers taking their cattle to London. This was probably the main reason why the Swan was established here and named after the swans which used to frequent the pond. The first reference to the property is from 1710 when it was called Mellors. By 1747 there are references to 'the sign of the White Swan'.[183] Apart from supplying spirits, wines and beers, it also provided board and lodgings, and the nearby barn and outbuildings supplied stabling and storage. There was also a smithy and a wheelwright's. The property came with 20 acres of land which lay to the rear. The Swan (the appendage White seems to have fallen out of use early in its history) was purchased in 1816 by Henry Lambert, a brewer from Writtle. This was a family business and eventually became part of the Writtle Brewery Company. Several decades later the Swan was purchased by Russell's Gravesend Brewery. In the earlier part of the nineteenth century, for over 20 years the licensees were Henry Charge and then his widow, Mary. Charge was also a wheelwright. After their time, like the Eagle Inn opposite, the Swan had a succession of licensees.

With the advent of the railways and shorter working hours, the countryside became the destination for city dwellers seeking fresh air on their day-off. The Swan became a popular stop-off for cyclists, walkers and visitors arriving by omnibus. One licensee, George Powe (who we first met at the Guardsman [19]), encouraged 'works outings' and 'beanfeast' parties from London. One such outing was for 70 employees of the Stratford Soap Works. They arrived in several horse-drawn carriages. After amusing themselves with games, they sat down to a dinner served in the adjacent barn which was decorated with evergreens, flowers and bunting.[184] Another annual outing was for the employees of Lion, Lion & Sons, boot and shoe manufacturers from Finsbury in London.[185]

Another organised outing which used the Swan as its headquarters involved a large party of boys from the east-end of London. It is not clear who the organisers were, probably a charity, but the arrival in a quiet rural parish of over eighty boys used to the poverty and grime of city life must have been a shock for members of both communities. On their arrival, five of the boys immediately set off for an orchard they had spied at Kumra Lodge [37] and filled their 'stomachs, handkerchiefs and pockets with delicious apples and pears'. But at the same time, they damaged many of the trees. Constable Medcalf was kept busy for the rest of the day tracking them down.[186]

The rowdy behaviour and minor thefts which accompanied some of these excursions resulted in many of the neighbours complaining to the police. They in turn raised their objections when it came to the renewal of Powe's license. At a court hearing in 1894 (having previously been warned in 1891), Powe was lucky to retain his license.[187] Shortly after he left the inn - probably because he was asked to do so by the brewery - and Henry Leeson took over.

Leeson had only been in occupancy for six weeks when in the early hours of 11 January 1895, a fire broke out. Within a short time, the entire timber building was destroyed. One of his servants had poured some methylated spirit into a lamp, lit it, but had left it too close to the bottle of methylated spirit which then caught light. Flames quickly spread throughout the property and the Leesons and the servant had to make a hasty escape. As their neighbours fought to stop the flames spreading to the outbuildings, a youth rode to Brentwood to call the fire brigade. The fire engine was delayed in arriving as suitable horses could not be found. By the time it did arrive, the house was destroyed and only a few of its contents had been salvaged. It was reported that the flames were seen for miles around.[188] The total value of the loss was estimated to be £400. Fortunately the property was insured. Within a year the Swan was rebuilt in brick, but now had a new licensee.

Fig. 82. Swan Inn c.1910.

In Fig. 82 above, the white swan sign has collapsed in the foreground. To the left is a barn, outbuildings and the smithy. On the right, the white building was a Mission Hall. It seems strange to have such a building next to a pub, but apart from appearing in two photographs, no further information can be found about it.

Glovers Farm [68] *d.*

Next to the Swan Inn was Glovers Farm, another timber building which would be consumed by a fire. The history of the farm is not known in any detail, but the name goes back to at least 1697. In 1839, it was acquired by a Charles Fox, and the property was described as a 'farm house, stable and outbuildings with 13 acres of land'.[189] By 1861, it was occupied by a tenant, Frederick Kent, and his wife, Sarah. Kent was an auctioneer, land agent and surveyor, and on occasions held auctions at the farm or next door in the Swan Inn. He also farmed the land.

They had nine children, but sadly, at least one did not live beyond infancy. In the Victorian home, the kitchen or a room with an open fire was a dangerous place for children. There are several examples of children in Kelvedon Hatch homes suffering terrible burns from unguarded fires and stoves. The Kent family were to suffer one such tragedy. They had left their children in the kitchen in the charge of a servant, when Arthur, their two-year-old, struck his head on a kettle and fell inside the fender pulling the kettle, full of boiling water, over himself. He was in agony until he died 24 hours later.[190] Despite this terrible event, the family remained at Glovers until at least 1880.

The next occupant of note is Matthias Clark and his wife, Frances. In 1892 they moved into the farmhouse as a newly married couple. It was his second marriage and Frances was over twenty years younger than him. His career had been as a miller, but now at the age of 61, he intended turning to farming. Their plans were thrown into confusion in March of the following year when the entire house was burnt down. Unfortunately, there are no detailed reports on the incident.[191] It was rebuilt in brick soon after and Matthias Clark lived there until his death in 1925 at the age of 95.

Poorhouse [69] *d.*

From Glovers Farm the tour goes along the Blackmore Road and towards its junction with the Ongar Road. On the left is a field, which until 1858 was common land; on the far side of this field stood a cottage. This was the poorhouse for Doddinghurst, owned and administered by the parish overseers. Unlike Kelvedon Hatch parish which sold off its poorhouse [11], Doddinghurst retained theirs and let it out to tenants at low rents. In 1851 it was occupied by Deborah Hammond, a widower, and her five young children; and Samuel Bull and his wife, Ann, both of whom were elderly. Both heads of the household were described in the census as paupers and they were fortunate to be living here instead of the workhouse. The property had been demolished by 1873.

Fig. 83. Swan Pond.
On the left is the rebuilt Glovers Farm [68], and in the distance, The Shepherd [71] and the Stores [72].

Cottage [70] *d.*

Returning along the Blackmore Road towards the Swan Pond, on the right lay a pair of semi-detached cottages owned by the Brizes estate. Nothing is known of their construction or history, and the census returns are difficult to interpret as to who the occupants were.

Hugh Justices / The Shepherd [71]

Opposite Swan Pond is The Shepherd pub (Fig. 84). Dating from the late-sixteenth century with later additions and alterations, this was a farmhouse until early in the 1830s when part of it became a beer shop, then a beer house, and later a public house. The property was originally known by the unusual name of Hugh Justices, possibly after an earlier owner. In 1819, the house and fields to the rear of it were purchased by a city merchant, John Atkins. His son, John Pelly Atkins, later inherited the property. In 1839, the property was described as 'a messuage, part of which is now used as a beer shop under the new act, [with] outbuildings, yard, garden, orchard and 24 acres [and] occupied by Henry Rule, yearly tenant.'[192] The act referred to above was the Beer House Act which allowed a householder to retail beer and cider from their house after payment of a small fee for a license. The idea was to popularise beer in place of spirits. The terms of their license would either permit consumption on the premises or would restrict the licensee to off-sales only. The word 'shop' in the description above, and in his listing in the 1851 trade directory, indicates that Rule's license only covered off-sales. By the 1860s, however, the word 'beer house' appears in the records. So by then we can assume the license had been extended.

At this time, though, the primary occupation of the inhabitants was still agricultural, and as the house was large, there were sometimes two families living in the house. In 1861, one of these families was the Goodwin family, Edward and Elizabeth. Elizabeth's occupation is described in the census as beer house keeper, while Edward's occupation is a shepherd. This is probably the origin of the name of pub.

In 1869, the Wine and Beer House Act changed the licensing controls for beer houses. Part of the effect of this was that many beer houses closed, while others were taken over by breweries. On the 18 May of that year, Atkins leased the property and land to C S Gray & Sons, brewers, for use as a beer house for a period of 21 years at a yearly rent of £33 (a lease which was later extended until the brewers purchased the property outright).

The first to hold the tenancy under CS Gray & Sons was John Maryon, he held it until at least 1889. He was followed by Walter Jordan who held it until 1902. If the census returns are representative of everyday life, then during the time of both these licensees, rooms were let out to several single men who were employed as agricultural workers.

The Shepherd was lucky to escape destruction by fire in 1873. Destroyed were a skittle shed and an adjoining storage shed which contained a tumbrel (a two-wheeled cart) and 25 ferrets (Maryon apparently bred and sold them). Fortunately, the Ongar Fire Brigade and many commoners were successful in stopping the fire spreading to the house.[193]

By 1905, the pub had become known locally as the 'Drum and Monkey'. Someone had obtained a mechanical toy of a monkey playing a drum, and this was housed in a glass case on the bar.[194]

The Stores [72]

Next to the Shepherd was a large brick-built house, part of which was a shop. There are references to it being called Boxhall, The Hatch and Fox Hatch House, but it features most often as The Stores. The date of its construction is not known, but a property on this site in 1781 was a licensed alehouse known as the Fox or Old Fox. After 1804, the name no longer appears in the license registers. In 1830, the building was described as 'a dwelling house with shop, granaries, stables, warehouse, cart lodge, [and] outbuildings, formerly known by the sign of the Old Fox.'[195] The property also came with the fields that lay to the rear of it. Throughout the nineteenth century until 1865, it was owned by the Box family and let out to tenants.

Fig. 84. The Shepherd in the 1920s.

Fig. 85. The Stores and the Shepherd c.1910.
On the right is The Shepherd, the large brick house is the Stores, and in the distance, the cottages [73] in Stocks Lane.

The first tenant we know of in great detail was Robert Skiggs, grocer and farmer. His father had also been a grocer and baker in Roxwell, while his brother was a tenant farmer in South Weald. From around 1839, Skiggs lived here with his wife, Sarah, and their six children. Living with them were two young men, aged twenty and twelve, who were working as shop assistants. For at least ten years, Skiggs also rented Glovers Farm [68]; he sub-let the farmhouse and farmed the land himself. Ten years later, Sarah had died and Skiggs was being assisted in the business by two of his children: Charles and Sarah. They also had three servants, two of whom were shop assistants. Skiggs died in 1858. Charles, now aged 21, took over the business helped by Sarah and his brother, Walter. Charles, however, was not a farmer, so the entire farming stock and equipment was sold and the tenancy on Glovers Farm ended.[196] The Skiggses had left the Stores by 1863, and the property was bought by the Brizes estate [28].

The next occupant was Samuel Whitnall. He carried on the business of grocer and dealer until he found himself in financial trouble in 1882 and was declared bankrupt. At least Whitnall had survived in business for almost twenty years, a later occupant, William Tennant, only lasted eleven months in the business and somehow managed to make a loss of £665. Not only that, he purchased the business using the proceeds of an inheritance his wife had come into, and now that was lost. He was also in debt to his father-in-law and brother-in-law who had loaned him £1000 to get him out of trouble with a previous employer over a matter of stolen money.[197] Many local businesses were creditors, including the licensees of the Swan Inn and The Shepherd, and they all found themselves receiving only 2s in the pound once the bankruptcy had been settled.

The next tenant of interest is shown in Fig. 86. Arthur Beardwell and his wife took up occupancy of the Stores in January 1915. On the back of the postcard he sent to a friend, he wrote: 'a lovely place with over ¼ an acre ground, any amount of fruit trees'.

Cottages [73]

The tour now goes along Blackmore Road and turns right into Stocks Lane. Fifty yards down Stocks Lane and on the left, was a pair of brick-built, semi-detached cottages, built after 1873 and before 1895 (Fig. 87). It is now one property. In 1911, both cottages were occupied by families with the same surname: Strong. Presumably they were related. One head of one of the households was a retired market gardener, while the other was an agricultural labourer.

Fig. 86. Arthur Beardwell outside the Stores.

Fig.87. Stocks Lane looking towards Blackmore Road, c.1925. On the right are two new wooden bungalows, the cottages [73], and in the distance, Stocks Cottages [74].

Fig. 88. Lady in the stocks.

Copt Hall / Stocks Cottages [74] *d.*

Returning to the Blackmore Road junction, on the same side of the road and overlooking the junction were two adjoining cottages. They probably dated from the late-eighteenth century. In 1861 they were both called Copt Hall, but by the end of the century, they were called Stocks Cottages. Reported to have been demolished by 1927, a watercolour painting of the cottages was made before they were demolished. It shows two adjoining cottages, and judging by their architecture, the right-hand one was added at a later date. They had black weather-boarding, white window frames and red tile roofs.[198] They were occupied by agricultural workers who included the Adams and Crabb families (1841-71); and in 1911, the right-hand cottage was occupied by Charles Porter, a boot and shoe repairer. His workshop was a shed attached to the side of the cottage (as recorded on the back of the painting).

The Stocks

The tour now finishes on the north side of this junction, by the stocks. Their early history is not known. In the 1930s they were estimated to be at least two hundred years old, but this was before the technique of dendrochronology came into use. The stocks were removed by the highways department of the Ongar District Union in 1935 so that some of the timbers could be renewed - much to the anger of local people and a local antiquarian

Fig. 89. Unfortunately, it is not known who this is, but judging by his age, he could easily have been born in the 1820s.

who alleged they were 'ripped out' without any care for their historic value. It is not known when they were returned, but by 1947 they had again been taken down, repaired and parts replaced. In the recent past they have again been repaired and moved to a small green space opposite their original location.

At the turn of the century when the cycle craze was in full flow, Kelvedon Hatch and Doddinghurst were on popular cycle routes. One route suggested by the Pall Mall Gazette started at Chadwell Heath and visited Navestock, Kelvedon Hatch, Blackmore, and finished at Greensted Church. Of Kelvedon Hatch it said, '…which brings the explorer to the scattered village of Kelvedon Hatch, a thoroughly English village, with the weather-boarded cottages and projecting red-brick chimney-breasts.'[199] The stocks became a popular stopping-off point for cyclists. They would all take turns in posing in the stocks while their friends took their photograph. The well-trodden earth in the picture left (Fig. 88) is evidence of this.

After 1920

This now concludes the tour of Kelvedon Hatch 1840 - 1920. After 1920, many small plots of land were sold-off for the building of bungalows, particularly in the Stocks Lane and Blackmore Road area. Later came council housing; and then providing the biggest impact of all, the housing estates of the 1960s and 1970s. The once scattered parish has now grown into the nucleated village we see today. Despite all these changes to the village, this tour shows that there are many historic houses and landscape features still to be seen in the parish.

Selected Bibliography

The National Archives

> Census Enumerators' Books 1841-1911 for Kelvedon Hatch and Doddinghurst

Essex Record Office

> Tithe maps and Ordnance Survey maps for Kelvedon Hatch and Doddinghurst
>
> Kelvedon Hall and Doddinghurst Hall manorial records
>
> Kelvedon Hatch and Doddinghurst church registers
>
> Property deeds and miscellaneous parish records, and sales catalogue for the Kelvedon Hall estate
>
> Chelmsford Chronicle and Essex Standard

British Library Newspaper Collection

> The British Newspaper Archive url: britishnewspaperarchive.co.uk
>
> Romford Library

Author's Collection

> St Nicholas' Church Parish Magazines: 1893, 1896-98, 1902

Selected Secondary Sources

Powell W. R. (Editor), Victoria County History: Essex: A History of the County of Essex: Volume 4: Ongar Hundred, (1956)

Farries Kenneth, Essex Windmills, Millers and Millwrights, Charles Skilton, 1981-88

Cowan Judy, Kelvedon Hatch: our village past and present, Old Village Pump Press 1984

Cowan Judy, A Domesday village: Kelvedon Hatch revisited and the Wrights of Kelvedon Hall, Old Village Pump Press, 1986

Fitch John Page, Glyn Jefferys, A Glimpse of Yesteryear in Kelvedon Hatch, Kelvedon Hatch Primary School, 1979

Notes

Abbreviations used:

ERO - Essex Record Office (references from their online catalogue: SEAX)

TNA - The National Archives

CC - Chelmsford Chronicle

EN - Essex Newsman

ES - Essex Standard

ET - Essex Times

PM - Kelvedon Hatch Parish Magazine published by St Nicholas's Church

1 CC 26 November 1841

2 Essex Place-names Project. Internet website accessed 25.2. 2014 URL: http://www.essex.ac.uk/history/esah/essexplacenames/index.aspa and A Dictionary of British Place Names, David Mills, 2011, Oxford University Press

3 Feet of Fines for Essex

4 Lay Subsidy of Essex

5 The Times 18 October 1831

6 Fitch

7 Memories of Malcolm Gower (1912-2013) in discussions with the author. Several times he was told by villagers of the anger that their father/grandfather felt over the enclosures.

8 ERO D/DU 233/11 and D/DU 233/2

9 ERO T/B 299/4 and 5

10 George P. (1994) Agricultural workers, their families and households: Kelvedon Hatch, Essex, 1851-1891. Final Project Report for Open University degree course DA 301.

11 ERO Kelvedon Hatch Register 1559-1695 D/P 296/1/1

12 Essex Countryside Magazine, September 1971, letter written by R. W. Porter, a former resident of Kelvedon Hatch.

13 CC 24 July 1863

14 Farries

15 ERO Sale/a279

16 EN 30 June 1888

17 Fitch

18 ERO Sale/a279

19 CC 08 September 1893

20 Kelvedon Hatch: Charities, Victoria County History

21 ERO T/A 592/3

22 ERO Sale/a279

23 Fitch

24 ET 9 July 1873 is an example.

25 CC 25 May 1883

26 ERO D/DU 1782

27 ERO T/P 188/3 These accounts of WWI are taken from the records of the Revd Reeve of Stondon Massey who kept a journal on the events of the time.

28 London 1914 – 1917 The Zeppelin Menace by Ian Castle, Osprey Publishing, 2008

29 Rural Life in England in the First World War by Pamela Horn, 1984, Gill and MacMillan

30 ERO T/P 188/3 As told to the Rev. Reeve of Stondon Massey.

31 CC 23 June 1916

32 ERO Sale/a279

33 House of Commons Papers, Digest of Parochial Returns made to the Select Committee appointed to inquire into the Education of the Poor, 1819

34 House of Commons Papers. Education Enquiry, Abstract of the Answers and Returns made pursuant to an address of the House of Commons, 24 May 1833

35 CC 05 July 1850

36 ERO D/P 30/28/18

37 Minutes of the Committee of Council on Education Correspondence, Financial Statements, etc., and Reports by Her Majesty's Inspectors of Schools, Volume 1, 1848

38 Minutes of the Committee of Council on Education Her Majesty's Inspector of Schools 1852/1853

39 ET 20 January 1875

40 EN 22 November 1879

41 Kelvedon Hatch School Log Book in the archives of Kelvedon Hatch Community Primary School.

42 PM 1893, 1896-98

43 ERO D/P 296/8/2

44 ERO D/F 63/1/16/23

45 ERO D/F 63/1/16/23

46 ERO Sale/a279

47 A Geography of Agricultural Bankruptcy in Late Victorian England and Wales, P.J. Perry, Agricultural History Review XX (1972)

48 EN 23 November 1889

49 CC 22 November 1889

50 CC 03 September 1909

51 PM 1897

52 CC 23 July 1897
53 CC 10 June 1898
54 ET 9 August 1879
55 ERO D/DU 1782/14
56 ET 3 May 1878
57 CC 05 June 1896
58 Fund raising leaflet published 1893, in the author's possession.
59 EN 11 November 1893
60 CC 10 December 1897
61 PM 1896-97
62 PM 1893
63 EN 01 June 1907
64 ERO D/P 296/30/2
65 ET 2 May 1877
66 ET 15 November 1878
67 EN 24 April 1874
68 ET 17 May 1876
69 ET 9 September 1871
70 PM August 1896
71 ERO Sale/a279
72 CC 29 August 1834
73 CC 20 August 1880
74 CC 08 October 1886
75 CC 09 June 1882
76 EN 19 November 1932
77 ERO SALE/A504
78 ERO 63/1/5/14
79 ERO D/DU 233/2
80 CC 06 April 1866
81 CC 12 March 1847
82 ES 26 September 1855
83 CC 21 May 1875
84 ES 05 August 1874
85 ERO Sale/a279
86 CC 07 February 1868

87 ERO D/DU 1478/1

88 ES 12 April 1834

89 EN 13 September 1884

90 CC 1 September 1893

91 EN 23 November 1895, provides additional particulars in a letting notice: 'three reception rooms, kitchen, scullery, six bedrooms, stabling, groom's room, coachhouse, cart sheds, and standing in 2 acres of garden, paddock and orchard.'

92 Fitch

93 CC 31 December 1852

94 ES 25 June 1852

95 CC 25 June 1852

96 EN 05 July 1887

97 CC 14 March 1913

98 ERO D/Ron 5/2/8

99 CC 07 February 1873

100 EN 25 February 1899

101 EN 25 February 1899

102 CC 17 January 1902

103 ERO D/Ron 5/2/4

104 CC 26 April 1907

105 ERO D/P 296/30/1

106 CC 16 March 1877

107 ERO D/P 296/8/2

108 CC 26 October 1895

109 EN 08 June 1878

110 ERO D/DXa 24

111 ET 13 February 1878

112 ET 28 June 1876

113 The Standard 26 January 1883

114 ERO D/P 296/8/2

115 ERO J/P 2/1 and J/P 2/2

116 PM 1902

117 CC 24 July 1896

118 Taunton Courier and Western Advertiser 4 March 1891

119 EN 27 May 1882

120 ERO D/DU 1782/14

121 CC 07 March 1834

122 ERO D/DU 1782/14

123 CC 08 June 1923

124 ET 11 October 1879

125 CC 01 March 1895

126 CC 18 June 1880

127 CC 28 January 1881

128 Kelvedon Hatch School Log Book in the archives of Kelvedon Hatch Community Primary School.

129 CC 11 May 1860

130 ERO D/DU 1782/14

131 CC 07 June 1929

132 ES 07 April 1854

133 EN 11 September 1880

134 EN 20 November 1886

135 EN 4 August 1877

136 ERO Q/SMc 11 1885, CC 30 October 1885

137 TNA WO97 series, Royal Hospital Chelsea: Soldiers Service Documents

138 TNA WO97 series, Royal Hospital Chelsea: Soldiers Service Documents

139 CC 9 December 1887

140 EN 6 December 1887

141 ERO Sale/a279

142 CC 3 September 1886

143 EN 22 August 1885

144 The Scotsman 25 May 1894

145 Royal Agricultural Society Journal, 1891, quoted in the Agrarian History of England and Wales, EJT Collins, page 174.

146 The Parishioner's Legal Adviser; Containing the Various Duties of Churchwardens, Overseers, Etc 1820. Internet website accessed 21.12.2013: Google Books.

147 ERO 296/8/2

148 CC 1 April 1881

149 EN 13 February 1882

150 CC 03 January 1845

151 Morning Post 19 December 1865

152 The Times 26 November 1840

153 Australian National University, National Centre of Biography. Internet website accessed 26.1.2014. Pastoral pioneers of South Australia Vol. 1 by R. Cockburn ISBN 0 86946 088 9 URL: http://ncb.anu.edu.au

154 CC 15 October 1875

155 EN 2 February 1884

156 Fitch

157 Note in the parish registers 1750 by George Kelly, the curate.

158 ERO D/CP 47/1

159 Berkshire Chronicle 14 August 1869

160 CC 19 December 1873

161 PM 1901

162 PM 1893-1895

163 ERO Q/SR 81/25

164 CC 3 September 1909

165 ERO Sale/a279

166 CC 25 September 1885

167 CC 19 February 1897

168 EN 7 November 1903 and CC 3 August 1923

169 The Times 22 June 1900 and EN 23 June 1900

170 ERO D/DFa E34

171 Morning Post 24 April 1829

172 The Times 25 April 1842

173 Every secondary source states it was demolished in 1837. Some suggest it was after a fire. It is clear from this advertisement, however, that it was demolished after 1842.

174 ERO Q/Rum 2/36

175 CC 19 November 1858

176 ERO D/CP 47/1

177 ERO Sale/a279

178 ES 5 April 1879 and 3 May 1879

179 Poem supplied to the author by a descendant of George Littlechild.

180 CC 20 January 1882

181 CC 7 July 1905

182 PM 1893

183 ERO D/DCh T43

184 EN 21 July 1888

185 CC 30 June 1893

186 EN 11 August 1894

187 CC 31 August 1894

188 CC 11 January 1895

189 ERO D/DPg/T4

190 CC 21 February 1862

191 CC 18 March 1892

192 ERO D/DPg/T4

193 ET 9 March 1873

194 Memories of Jane Sugden in author's possession and CC 27 October 1905.

195 ERO DDHt T87/5

196 CC 21 January 1859

197 CC 4 August 1893

198 ERO I/Mp 249/1/7

199 Pall Mall Gazette September 1899

Lightning Source UK Ltd.
Milton Keynes UK
UKHW020108160321
380381UK00006B/1264